Invincible Love, Invisible War

Eleanor Lewis

with Pat Harley and Linda Sweeney

BIG DREAM
MINISTRIES

ISBN 13: 978-1-932199-15-4
ISBN 10: 1-932199-15-2

Cover design by Melissa Swanson

The anecdotal illustrations in this book are true to life and are included with the permission of the persons involved.

Unless otherwise identified, all Scripture quotations in this publication are taken from the *New American Standard Bible* (NASB), © The Lockman Foundation 1960, 1962, 1963, 1968, 1971, 1972, 1973, 1975, 1977, 1995. Additional versions used: *The Living Bible* (TLB), copyright © 1971, used by permission of Tyndale House Publishers, Inc., Wheaton, IL 60189, all rights reserved; and the *King James Version* (KJV).

contents

welcome!

As the four teachers of *The Amazing Collection: The Bible, Book by Book* (Pat Harley, Margie Reuther, Linda Sweeney, and I) studied and taught the entire Bible in our video series, we were overwhelmed by the powerful love story of God. The Bible is not only history; it is His story. Although the Bible is about Him, it is also about us, the objects of His affection. Therefore, in addition to God's love, we were confronted with our wars with sin, Satan, and the world's influence.

Even though the Bible was written over a period of about 1,500 years by over forty authors, there is a unity that can only be explained as supernatural. There is a consistent message that God loves us and that although life is a series of battles, He desires for us to live in victory.

This study, based on an outline Pat, Linda, and I developed for a seminar, presents the big picture of God's love and His plan to give you a future and a hope! It also gives a biblical perspective on the battles we face. As you work through each lesson, savor the goodness and greatness of God, knowing He can be your Sovereign King, your Wisdom, your Judge, your Savior, your Teacher, and your Victorious King!

Eleanor Lewis

Helps for using this study

Invincible Love, Invisible War may be used in groups or by individuals. The DVDs provide additional information not found in the workbook and are a springboard for deeper understanding and study of the written materials. The student is encouraged to engage daily in the Scriptures. The study moves through the Bible sequentially, as the goal is for the student to understand the big picture of the entire Bible. Though this is a unique way to study, its rewards will be great.

If doing the study alone

The individual student has the advantage of doing the workbook at a rate that is comfortable and allows time for deeper study. However, this method also requires the greatest amount of self-discipline. The DVD should be watched at the beginning of each of the six sections, followed by daily time in the workbook and Scriptures. The review questions that follow each section should be answered in writing.

If doing the study in a small group

The first session, The Old Testament History DVD, should be watched as a group. (There is a page for DVD Notes at the beginning of each section.) The DVD is followed by discussion of the questions on page 22. The following week, the students are encouraged to complete the homework and come prepared to discuss their answers at the beginning of the next week's session.

The facilitator can guide the discussion of the past week's homework by using the Review/Discussion Questions at the end of that week's study and the Love & War Questions found within the daily homework. Regardless of group size, review often so you can truly learn for life. Follow the discussion time by viewing the next DVD in the series. As time allows, end each session with a brief discussion of the DVD and prayer.

If doing the study in a large group

It is helpful to divide a large group into smaller groups of eight to ten. A facilitator will be needed for each small group. Follow the guidelines for small groups above.

The seventh week

Though this is a six-lesson study, a seventh week is needed for discussion of the New Testament Prophecy homework. It is also helpful to review the material from sessions 1–6. A sharing time of what the course has taught or meant to the students can also be meaningful.

▶ **Please note:** For facilitator helps, download the Small Group Leaders' Training Guide. Leader helps are found on pages 37–64 of the brochure. Go to http://www.theamazingcollection.com/PDFs/TAC_Guidebook.pdf

introduction

A Personal Story of
Love and *War*

THE RELENTLESS ENEMY OF ADDICTION

The first shot of my war was fired when I was just eight years old. I was one of those kids so desperate for acceptance that I would do almost anything to fit in. Moving every two to three years provided ample opportunity to hone my skills of social deception.

Shortly after we moved from Seattle, Washington, to Atlanta, Georgia, I met the other boys my age in the neighborhood, and my act began. "Sports? Yeah, I love sports, and I'm very good at them." Deceit flowed effortlessly from my lips and soon earned me an invitation into the inner sanctum of boyhood — the tree house. I planted my foot proudly on the bottom rung of the ladder and began my climb to acceptance. When my head popped through the floor, I was filled with such a rush. What I saw was like nothing I had ever experienced.

The owner of this tree house, Fred, had older brothers who had acted as decorators. Their choice of wallpaper was pages from *Playboy* and *Penthouse*! At the age of eight, I was exposed to pornography, and it became my enemy for the next twenty-four years. This enemy struck by surprise, and, trust me, the shock and awe of the attack far surpasses any military power. Viewing pornography feels good, which is the key to its destructive power. Instead of repulsing a person, porn draws him in so he wants more. In fact, he will willingly finance the very war that damages him and others along the way.

I felt unlovable, and the more I lied in an effort to create the right mask to gain acceptance, the more unlovable I felt. It's an insidious cycle, isn't it? Maybe you know it yourself. I lied to everyone. When I brought home from school my first 99 instead of 100, my father said, "What — couldn't get 100?" I was devastated and learned that anything less than perfection would be unacceptable and subject to ridicule. So I began forging my parents' names in the third grade! This behavior also sent me to the tree house to cope with the guilt and shame of lying.

I hated competition. Competition opened up the possibility of defeat, so in my mind, competition was only imperfection with witnesses. One day my dad and I were playing basketball and I kept losing. Finally I collapsed on the driveway in tears. Retrieving my last blocked shot, Dad yelled, "You are such a baby! I don't even like you right now!" He then threw the basketball at me, hitting me in the face and knocking my head on the concrete. He walked in the house, and we never spoke about it again. Can you guess what I did? I ran to the tree house because what I found there made me feel better. The images of women provided the illusion of acceptance I so desperately craved.

This pattern became deeply entrenched in the programming of my brain. Where there was pain, there was porn. This continued until I was old enough to become sexually active and put into practice all I had been learning from pornography. However, guarding my image, I was always at church. I was a leader in the youth group and was selected to deliver the sermons on youth day. People had no idea I was living a grand lie. They saw and praised the mask I wore, which oddly enough made me feel worse. They didn't know the real me, and I was terrified to let them find out. I believed that if anyone knew where I had been, what I had done, and what I had thought, there was *no way* they could love me.

I felt that way about God, too. I was sure He could not love me and that He was sitting on a distant throne glaring at me with disapproval, ready to throw a basketball in my face. The ravages of this war had distorted my view of love and of God.

The war with this enemy I had chosen continued to rage into my marriage, but I convinced myself I was being faithful since it was only porn. So I had a wife who had married my mask but not the real me.

I had a view of God in which He demanded a perfection I was incapable of and was waiting to throw things at me when I screwed up. And I had a mother who was a well-known Bible teacher and, since my dad had died of cancer, was now married to evangelical legend Cliff Barrows (no pressure there!). I was convinced if any of them found out, they would leave me.

Here's the thing about addiction to sex and porn: It is an intimacy disorder. I so desperately wanted to be loved and accepted but believed that was impossible. Finally the day came that I could not take it anymore. I knew I had to risk vulnerability to gain intimacy. I confessed to my wife all I had done and how I had lied to her. I braced for the assault I expected, but it did not come. We both began counseling to help us deal with our issues and to better understand ourselves and each other. After being honest with my wife, I told my mother and stepfather. They didn't run from me either. Wow! I could not believe it!

I was learning that not only did my spouse and family love the real me, but God loved the real me as well. He knew all about me and loved me anyway! The war I fought was not with God but rather with my distorted view of God. He sees me not only as I am but also as I am going to be. I don't have to earn His love. In fact, I could never earn His love! Philip Yancey's definition of grace has it right — there's nothing you can do to make God love you any less, and there's nothing you can do to make God love you any more.

I had resolved countless times to stop turning to pornography. I would plead with God to give me the strength to fight this battle. I would beg Him to take the desire from me, but He would not. He was waiting for me to desire Him and His glory above myself. When I did that, He rushed in to rescue me with His sovereign, empowering grace.

It is not making resolutions or fighting harder that wins a spiritual battle. It is only surrender that ends the war. I had to surrender to my loving heavenly Father, who does not waste anything, including our pain. I now pastor a unique community of people willing to be transparent in their struggles. God has also given me a weekly satellite radio show to introduce people in the throes of the battle to the truth of the gospel so they, too, can experience God's victory by being transformed into the likeness of Jesus Christ. I lived for twenty-four years convinced that I was unlovable. I finally learned I was wrong.

The LORD your God is in your midst,
　　A victorious warrior.
　　He will exult over you with joy,
　　He will be quiet in His love (some versions say, "He will renew you in His love"),
　　He will rejoice over you with shouts of joy. (Zephaniah 3:17)

Your personal battle may not be with pornography, but in the next few weeks we will see that we all have battles that come in many different forms. We will also see that Almighty God desires to live in our midst as our victorious *warrior*, to renew us in His *love*. Love and war — in the Word of God and in our daily lives, we find a constant struggle between the two. Everyone desires love, yet the war we seek to avoid is all around us.

God says,

　　I have loved you with an everlasting love;
　　Therefore I have drawn you with lovingkindness. (Jeremiah 31:3)

But He also tells us, "Put on the full armor of God, so that you will be able to stand firm against the schemes of the devil" (Ephesians 6:11).

Why would a God who loves us give us armor if we weren't in a war? Do our life struggles and defeats mean He does not love us? Regardless of your age, all your life the news has reported wars taking place in various parts of the world. Maybe you have been the victim of crime or have witnessed violence in your community. Perhaps in your own home you've been a bystander or active participant in battles of words or quiet hostility. And what about the ongoing war in our own hearts against selfishness, fear, anger, and temptation?

In the midst of these wars, the Bible is God's love letter to us. The Word of God helps us understand the depth of God's love and the reasons we resist receiving it. It reveals the forces standing in the way of an intimate relationship with Him. To fight the battles in our lives, He has given us armor and one offensive weapon, revealed in the book of Ephesians: "the sword of the Spirit, which is the word of God" (6:17).

Your weapon, the Word of God, is truly unique. First, the Bible differs from any other book in the sense that it is actually a library made up of sixty-six books of history, poetry, self-help, biography, law, and wisdom. Over forty authors from many walks of life composed it, including two kings, a fisherman, a doctor, a sheep breeder, a cup bearer, and a priest.

The Bible was written over a period of 1,500–1,600 years on three continents — Asia, Africa, and Europe — and in three languages — Hebrew, Greek, and Aramaic. Yet there is one consistent theme throughout because God is the same yesterday, today, and forever! The Bible claims that all Scripture was inspired by God, or God breathed (2 Timothy 3:16), and that none of it was written as an act of human will but by men who were moved by the Holy Spirit and spoke from God (2 Peter 1:21).

The Bible was the first book to be mechanically printed and is the most widely distributed book ever written. It is the best-documented text from the ancient world, and yet many people seldom read it! Though ancient, the Bible is relevant for us today. It reveals the battles we face daily and tells us who the Enemy is and how he operates. It also helps us know and understand the character, work, and power of our Defender. It not only instructs us on how to live in the battle, but it also assures us ultimate victory!

Moses made a bold statement about the Word of God: "For it is not an idle word for you; indeed it is your life" (Deuteronomy 32:47). Jesus reiterated the same idea when He said, "Man shall not live on bread alone, but on every word that proceeds out of the mouth of God" (Matthew 4:4). The Bible is not made up of idle words; indeed it is your life!

Through our study of God's Word we will discover how deeply we are loved, how mighty our battle is, and how we can endure to the end.

▶ Please look at **The Bible** chart on page 15. To grasp the flow of the Bible it is helpful to break it down into six divisions:

- Old Testament History
- Old Testament Writings
- Old Testament Prophecy
- New Testament History
- New Testament Writings
- New Testament Prophecy

Note the three key words: history, writings, and prophecy.

▶ *The History books* tell us how God's love was rejected and the war ensued, what the battle is about, and, most important, who our Defender is and how He has already won the victory over sin.

▶ *The Writings* give us wisdom to protect and defend us. They enable us to believe rightly so we will live as we should, and they equip us to stand firm.

▶ *Prophecy* tells us what has happened and warns us what will happen in the future, including the final war that will bring total victory!

In *Invincible Love, Invisible War* we will study one of these six Bible divisions each week. We will begin week 1 by looking at the seventeen Old Testament History books to understand how the Old Testament history of love and war applies to us today.

The following resources will help you as you work through this study:

▶ The **map** on page 16 shows the area of the world where all the events we read about in the Old Testament took place. Today that area would include the countries of Israel, Syria, Iran, Iraq, Jordan, Saudi Arabia, and Egypt.

▶ The **Chronological Relationship of the Old Testament Books** chart on page 17 will be very helpful to you as you study the Bible. The middle section shows the seventeen Old Testament History books.

- The **larger boxes** of Genesis through Nehemiah are books that record history *in chronological order*. In other words, the events in Exodus follow the events in Genesis, the events in Numbers follow the events in Exodus, and so on.

- The **smaller boxes** of Leviticus, Deuteronomy, Ruth, 1 Chronicles, 2 Chronicles, and Esther are history books also; however, they *do not advance the story in time* but rather add additional information to the narrative. For instance, the book of Ruth tells of a family and an event that took place during the time period of Judges.

THE BIBLE

OLD TESTAMENT HISTORY

17 Books
Genesis – Esther

GOD OUR SOVEREIGN KING

OLD TESTAMENT WRITINGS

5 Books
Job – Song of Solomon

GOD OUR WISDOM

OLD TESTAMENT PROPHECY

17 Books
Isaiah – Malachi

GOD OUR JUDGE

NEW TESTAMENT HISTORY

5 Books
Matthew – Acts

JESUS OUR SAVIOR

NEW TESTAMENT WRITINGS

21 Books
Romans – Jude

JESUS OUR TEACHER

NEW TESTAMENT PROPHECY

1 Book
Revelation

JESUS OUR VICTORIOUS KING

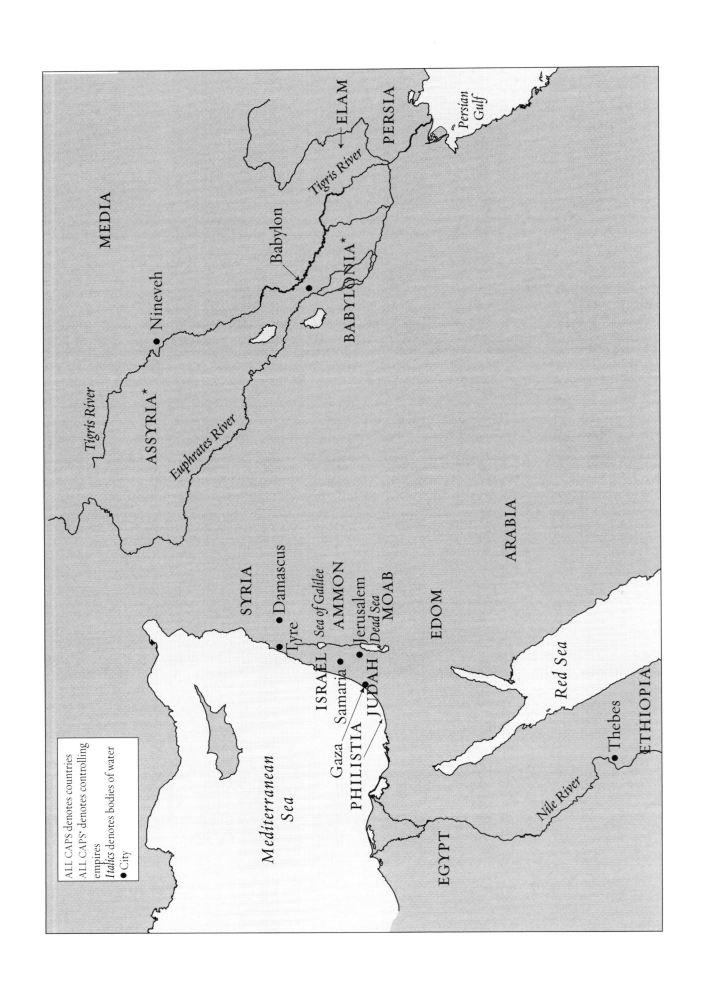

CHRONOLOGICAL RELATIONSHIP OF THE OLD TESTAMENT BOOKS

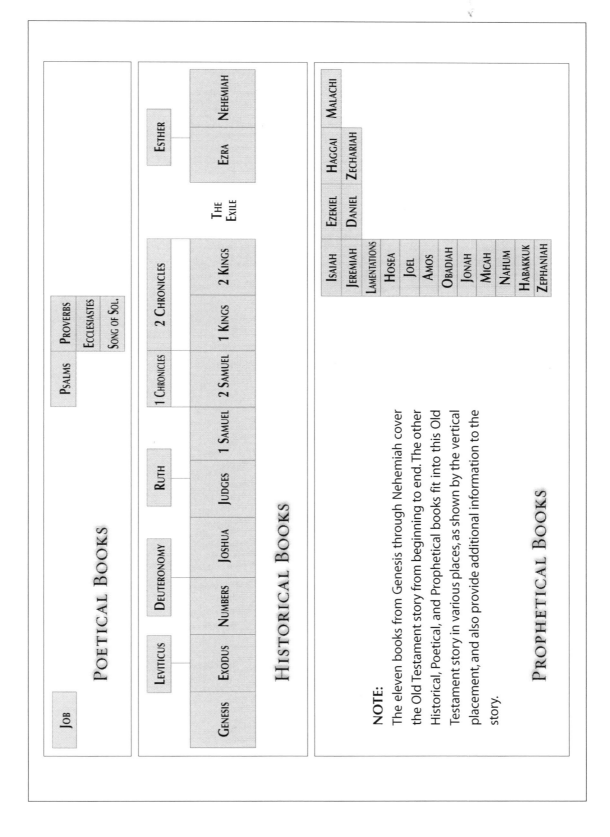

POETICAL BOOKS

JOB

PSALMS

PROVERBS
ECCLESIASTES
SONG OF SOL.

HISTORICAL BOOKS

GENESIS | EXODUS | NUMBERS | JOSHUA | JUDGES | 1 SAMUEL | 2 SAMUEL | 1 KINGS | 2 KINGS

LEVITICUS

DEUTERONOMY

RUTH

1 CHRONICLES | 2 CHRONICLES

THE EXILE

ESTHER

EZRA | NEHEMIAH

PROPHETICAL BOOKS

ISAIAH | EZEKIEL | HAGGAI | MALACHI

JEREMIAH | DANIEL | ZECHARIAH

LAMENTATIONS
HOSEA
JOEL
AMOS
OBADIAH
JONAH
MICAH
NAHUM
HABAKKUK
ZEPHANIAH

NOTE:

The eleven books from Genesis through Nehemiah cover the Old Testament story from beginning to end. The other Historical, Poetical, and Prophetical books fit into this Old Testament story in various places, as shown by the vertical placement, and also provide additional information to the story.

#1
old testament
history

god our sovereign king

#1 DVD Notes

Introduction
Discussion/Review Questions for DVD #1

(Use for group discussion or personal review after watching DVD #1 Old Testament History)

1. What is the most important thing you learned from the DVD teaching?

2. What did you learn from the Personal Story of Love and War? (Tal's story "The Enemy of Addiction" on the DVD is repeated on page 11 of this workbook.)

3. What did you learn about the Word of God?

4. What did you learn about God's relationship with man?

5. What did you learn about your enemies?

6. What did you learn about yourself and the battles you face?

7. Name the six divisions of the Bible (see chart on page 15).

A Personal Story of
Love and *War*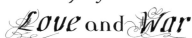

THE ENEMY OF FEAR

Growing up in a wonderful loving home and attending a small church, I learned Bible stories about Jesus but failed to learn about a relationship with Him. Instead I came to believe that God was like Santa Claus: Occasionally I could call on Him for some of the really important things in life, like helping me get a good grade on a test, but I did not think about God very often.

When I was twenty-one years old I was attending graduate school and was six weeks away from marrying a young man I had been in love with since I was fifteen. I lived in an apartment with another girl and one night woke up with a hand over my mouth, a knife pressed into my neck, and a man with a mask sitting on the side of my bed. I was sure I was going to die.

Crying out to God, I asked the "Santa" in heaven to send help immediately. But God chose not to answer in the way I thought He should. My roommate was locked in a closet and I was brutally assaulted. When my attacker walked out of my apartment, whatever faith in God I had walked out with him. I understood there was a battle between good and evil going on in my community, and it was a battle I could not conquer or control.

Because He did not rescue me that night, I felt God must not be very powerful. Or perhaps He did not love me enough to intervene. Or maybe He was not even aware that I needed help. As a result, God and I parted company. I married and moved on. I did not bother God, and as far as I could tell, He did not bother me.

During this time our country was at war in Vietnam. My peers were going to war and many were not coming home alive. Every evening the news brought pictures of great destruction, suffering, and pain. And I saw another battle taking place — a battle among the nations.

After ten years of marriage, I was facing more misery than I could ever have imagined. Our relationship had deteriorated until there was no longer any trust, love, or devotion between us. I went into a deep depression and even thought of ending my life. Now there was another battle raging. It was within my marriage.

Those years were lived in constant fear. I feared being attacked again. I feared the dark. I feared being alone. I feared everything. Although I fought to do so, I could not conquer my fears.

So there was a battle in my community, a battle in the nations, a battle in my marriage, and a battle in my own heart. In absolute hopelessness, I cried out to the God of my youth. He had been waiting for me all that time, and He answered.

Shortly after I prayed for help, God opened the door for me and my husband to attend a Bible study. It was through His Word that God began to heal my marriage and reveal Himself to me in a powerful way. He also began to heal my heart and my fears through a relationship with my Savior and victorious warrior, Jesus Christ.

old testament history

Overview

The LORD, the LORD God, compassionate and gracious, slow to anger, and abounding in lovingkindness and truth. (Exodus 34:6)

▶ The seventeen Old Testament History books show God as our **Sovereign King**.

The Personal Story of Love and War "The Enemy of Fear" on page 23 reminds us that fear is a weapon of the Enemy and a battle we will all face. However, God our Sovereign King tells us, "There is no fear in love; but perfect love casts out fear" (1 John 4:18). Only God has perfect love, for He is "compassionate and gracious, slow to anger, and abounding in lovingkindness and truth."

The Old Testament History books of Genesis through Esther make up about one-third of the Bible. The length of time covered in the opening chapters of Genesis is unknown, but from Genesis chapter 12 to the end of Nehemiah is a time period of about 2,000 years.

Please look at the **Chronological Relationship of the Old Testament Books** chart on page 17. The first five books of history (Genesis — Deuteronomy) are called the *Pentateuch*, and they show us the beginning of all things. We see God's love and power in the story of Creation and man's war with rebellious pride. We see the beginning of sin, which led to languages and nations. These books also reveal God's choice of a family and His promise that they would become a great nation. God would give them land and they would produce a descendant who would bless the world.

The next seven books of history (Joshua — 2 Kings) are called *Kingdom Books*, and they tell how God's promised nation, Israel, conquered the land and became a kingdom. Israel demanded a human king, even though God was their king (making their nation a theocracy). God had warned them of the consequences of having a human king, but He gave them what they desired. (The lesson? Watch what you ask for because you might get it!) God also warned the people that their idolatry would be considered spiritual adultery. Worshiping anyone or anything but Him constituted unfaithfulness and would break their covenant with God and result in separation from Him. Because they did not listen to this warning, after about eight hundred years the nation of Israel was conquered and exiled from the land, just as God had warned.

The last five books of history (1 Chronicles — Esther) are called *Post-Exilic Books*. They tell how after seventy years in exile God miraculously returned the people He loved to their land to rebuild and restore it just as He had promised.

In a battle it is important to know your enemy. Let's learn a little about one of ours.

▶ Like man, Satan is a creation of God (Genesis 3:1); however, in pride, Satan desired the glory only God deserves. (Isaiah 14:13-14)

▶ Satan can tempt us or fill our hearts with evil thoughts or desires:
Satan stood up against Israel and moved David to number Israel. (1 Chronicles 21:1)

Jesus, full of the Holy Spirit, returned from the Jordan and was led around by the Spirit in the wilderness for forty days, being tempted by the devil. (Luke 4:1-2)

But Peter said, "Ananias, why has Satan filled your heart to lie to the Holy Spirit and to keep back some of the price of the land?" (Acts 5:3)

▶ Satan has a kingdom that is in conflict with God's kingdom:
Jesus said, "If Satan also is divided against himself, how will his kingdom stand? . . . But if I cast out demons by the finger of God, then the kingdom of God has come upon you (Luke 11:18,20).

▶ Satan is a ruler men can choose to follow:
For some have already turned aside to follow Satan. (1 Timothy 5:15)

They may come to their senses and escape from the snare of the devil, having been held captive by him to do his will. (2 Timothy 2:26)

Do not give the devil an opportunity. (Ephesians 4:27)

▶ Satan can cause illness or tribulation:
And there was a woman who for eighteen years had had a sickness caused by a spirit. [After healing her, Jesus said,] "And this woman . . . whom Satan has bound for eighteen long years, should she not have been released from this bond on the Sabbath day?" (Luke 13:11,16)

Do not fear what you are about to suffer. Behold, the devil is about to cast some of you into prison, so that you will be tested, and you will have tribulation for ten days. (Revelation 2:10)

▶ Satan is a liar and a murderer:
Jesus said to the Jews who were seeking to kill him, "You are of your father the devil, and you want to do the desires of your father. He was a murderer from the beginning, and does not stand in the truth because there is no truth in him. Whenever he speaks a lie, he speaks from his own nature, for he is a liar and the father of lies" (John 8:44).

▶ Satan's end has already been decreed by God:
The Sovereign King said, "Depart from Me, accursed ones, into the eternal fire which has been prepared for the devil and his angels" (Matthew 25:41).

What did you learn about Satan, your Enemy?

man's Battle Begins

▶ The seventeen Old Testament History books show God as our **Sovereign King**. They can be divided into three subsections:

    ▶ *Pentateuch:* Genesis, Exodus, Leviticus, Numbers, Deuteronomy
    ▶ *Kingdom Books:* Joshua, Judges, Ruth, 1 Samuel, 2 Samuel, 1 Kings, 2 Kings
    ▶ *Post-Exilic Books:* 1 Chronicles, 2 Chronicles, Ezra, Nehemiah, Esther

The Old Testament History Books, or first seventeen books of God's love letter explain the beginning of all things. They present the story of the sovereign Creator's desire to have an intimate relationship with the people He created. (Sometimes He refers to this relationship as a Father and child and other times as a marriage.) However, even when men disappoint God or run from Him, because of His invincible love He makes promises and provision for restoration.

A. Meet the loving Creator.
    1. List the ways God showed His love when creating mankind:
       a. Genesis 1:27-28

       b. Genesis 2:8-9,15

       c. Genesis 2:18,21-22

After creating a perfect home, God inhabited it with perfect people and animals. From the beginning, humans and animals were different. God breathed His own breath, or life, into men (Genesis 2:7), making them spiritual beings so that God, who is spirit (John 4:24), could have a personal relationship with them. He even spoke to them, giving them a job, or life purpose. However, His children were free to choose to obey or disobey God's plan.

2. What one command did God give (see Genesis 2:16-17)?

Because God is a loving Father, He gave His children the whole world, except the tree of the knowledge of good and evil. Obeying God would prove that man loved God, as God expressed in John 14:15: "If you love Me, you will keep My commandments."

B. Meet your Enemy.
1. Who tempted the first man and woman to disobey God and how (see Genesis 3:1,4-5)? (Revelation 12:9 says, "The serpent of old" is Satan.)

2. How did Adam and Eve respond to Satan's temptation and why (see Genesis 3:6)?

3. How did Satan's temptation of man in the garden in Genesis 3:5 mirror his own desire in Isaiah 14:14 when he said, "I will make myself like the Most High"?

Man's battles began by rejecting God's love. Now we are in a war waged on two battlefields: *within* and *without*. Peter warned about the battle within when he said to "abstain from fleshly lusts which wage war against the soul" (1 Peter 2:11). He also warned about the battlefield without when he said, "Your adversary, the devil, prowls around like a roaring lion, seeking someone to devour" (1 Peter 5:8). To be victorious in this battle of life, we must obey God's admonition to take up "the sword of the Spirit, which is the word of God" (Ephesians 6:17)!

C. There were and are consequences for rejecting God's love.
1. List the personal or human consequences of man's disobedience to God:
   a. Genesis 3:16

b. Genesis 3:17-18

c. Genesis 3:19 (What phrase is repeated in Genesis 5:5,8,11?)

2. List the consequences man's disobedience caused in his relationship with God:
   a. Genesis 3:8-10

   b. Genesis 3:22-24

Disobedience resulted in a more difficult life than God intended. Sin not only brought into the world shame, pain, and fear, but it also caused all of mankind to be separated from God and His provision of the Tree of Life. Sin always separates, and something always dies!

3. List the consequences man's disobedience caused to family relationships and society:
   a. Genesis 3:11-12

   b. Genesis 6:11-12

Sin not only separated us from God, but it also resulted in people's separation from one another. Adam and Eve blamed each other for their disobedience, and their son Cain murdered his brother, starting a wave of violence on the earth.

LOVE & WAR QUESTION: Which of the many consequences of sin most affects your life today, including your relationships with God and others?

D. Despite man's rebellion, God continued to provide for those He loved.

God made a promise to deal with sin. He promised to send a "seed," or descendant, who would crush the serpent, or Satan, though His own heel would be crushed in the process (Genesis 3:15).

1. Adam and Eve apparently were "clothed" with innocence, or righteousness. After their rebellion they lost this covering and were naked. How did God show His love (see Genesis 3:21)?

2. In spite of man's violence and corruption and God's promise to judge the earth by destroying it, how did God show His love (see Genesis 6:13-14; 7:1)?

God provided Noah and his family an ark of safety from the judgment of the flood. Here we see a principle of God that continues throughout His Word. Though God must judge disobedience, He always provides a way of escape for those who belong to Him.

After the flood, Noah's family got off the ark and grew in number. Though the corrupt earth had been judged, man's heart had not changed—it was still deceitful. Man's disobedience had brought lifelong and life-ending consequences. The war was still raging. However, God is a Sovereign King above all kings and rulers and He did not want to be separated from the people He loved. As we continue our study of the History books, God's plan and promise to send the "seed" to deal with Satan and end our sin-induced separation from God will unfold.

LOVE & WAR QUESTION: What have you learned about God, your Sovereign King?

REVIEW IT!
Disobedience always brings consequences.

god's victory begins

The History books of Genesis through Esther tell not only the beginning of our battle with Satan and sin but also the beginning of God's solution. After man disobeyed, God desired to renew us in His love; therefore, He chose Abraham to provide a way to victory. These books show the history of the nation of Israel from the time God called Abraham until four hundred years before Abraham's seed, or descendant, Jesus, was born.

A. God provides an answer to our battle with sin.

    1. God made an everlasting covenant with Abraham to be God to him and his descendants, to bless them, and to make their name great (Genesis 17:7). What else did God promise?

       a. Genesis 12:2

       b. Genesis 17:8

       c. Genesis 22:18 (see Galatians 3:16 for clarification on "your seed" or "one descendant")

God made a covenant with Abraham that promised:

  ▶ Abraham would become the father of a great nation.
  ▶ God would give that nation the land of Canaan.
  ▶ A descendant of Abraham and that nation would bless the whole earth.

B. Israel was to be the instrument of God's blessing in the world.

The Old Testament History books tell the story of Abraham's descendants. Through them an answer to life's battles would come. Abraham's grandson Jacob had twelve sons whose offspring became the twelve tribes of Israel! In spite of God's commands, this family did not keep themselves holy or separate from the wicked nations around them but instead behaved like them.

In His sovereign love, God moved Jacob's entire family of seventy to Egypt. Because the Egyptians loathed the Hebrew profession of shepherding, they would not have a relationship with the Hebrews (Genesis 43:32; 46:31-34). Therefore, God's people were not tempted to worship the Egyptians' false gods. Sometimes in order to keep us from being separated from Him, God works circumstances in our lives to separate us from temptations.

1. What happened during the 430 years the descendants of Jacob were in Egypt (see Exodus 1:8-11; 2:23-24)?

During their 430 years in Egypt (Exodus 12:40), God fulfilled His promise to Abraham to make him a great nation. While they were there, his extended family of seventy became a nation of several million. However, a new Pharaoh came to power and enslaved them. Still, even when our circumstances look bad, God is at work for our good.

During Israel's bondage, God raised up a great leader to deliver them. God prepared Moses for forty years in Pharaoh's palace, where he learned the ways of Egypt, and for forty years in the wilderness, where he learned to lead sheep. Through Moses God warned the Egyptians to let the Hebrews return to their land. When Pharaoh didn't release them, God used ten plagues to deliver His people out of Egypt.

2. What was the last plague against Egypt (see Exodus 11:4-5)?

3. What was the only thing that would save the Israelites from this plague of death (see Exodus 12:3-7,12-13)?

Once more in His love God provided a way out for His people. He decreed that the angel of death would pass over any house where the blood of the lamb had been applied to the doorpost. All men had to follow God's instruction to receive His provision. Although Christ, the seed God had promised to bless the whole world, had not yet arrived, He was foreshadowed by this Passover lamb, which would save anyone willing to personally apply its shed blood.

The New Testament tells us God "preached the gospel beforehand to Abraham, saying, 'All the nations will be blessed in you.' . . . The promises were spoken to Abraham and to his seed . . . that is, Christ" (Galatians 3:8,16).

C. Mt. Sinai prepared Israel for war.

After delivering Israel from Egypt through the Red Sea with a mighty miracle, God took them to Mt. Sinai to prepare this nation of former slaves to conquer and live in the land of Canaan. To accomplish this God gave Israel His laws and commandments.

1. The first four commandments given at Mt. Sinai deal with man's relationship with God. What did these laws require and why (see Exodus 20:3-5)?

2. Note that God calls Himself jealous. The *New Bible Dictionary* (Tyndale) says the word *jealous* means:

> A consuming single-minded pursuit of a good end. This positive usage is frequently associated with the marriage relationship, where a jealousy for the exclusiveness of the relationship is the necessary condition of its permanence. . . . Scripture also witnesses to a positive application of jealousy and finds in this idea a highly relevant term to denote God's holy zeal for the honor of His name and the good of His people who are bound to Him in the marriage of the covenant. In this sense the jealousy of God is of the essence of His moral character, a major cause for worship and confidence on the part of His people and a ground for fear on the part of His enemies.

God is jealous for an eternal, exclusive relationship with us for His honor and our good!

3. The last six commandments deal with man's relationship with men. We are to honor our parents. We are not to murder, commit adultery, steal, bear false witness, or covet. (Exodus 20:12-17) How do you see God's love in these commandments?

The first four commandments show us how to live right with God, and the last six show us how to live right with each other. God's laws were given after the people were delivered from bondage. God never intended for the law to save us but to show how a delivered people should live.

4. After giving them His commandments, what did God instruct the people to build? What three things did He say He would do in this place (see Exodus 25:8-9,22)?

5. What happened after the people completed construction of the tabernacle (see Exodus 40:35-38)?

God gave instructions for the building of a tabernacle (also called the sanctuary or tent of meeting). He desired to dwell in the midst of His people, so the tabernacle was kept at the center of the camp. From there God would meet with them, speak to them, and lead them. As they followed God He gave them victory over their enemies. God desires to be at the very center of our lives to speak to us and lead us as well.

LOVE & WAR QUESTION: God desired to live in the center of the Israelites' lives. What benefits would this kind of proximity provide you? How can you live this out?

6. Have you asked Jesus to live at the center of your life? If so, what do you remember about that time?

If you have never done so, now is a great time to tell God your need for Him. You might say something like this:

> Lord, thank You for loving me. I have rebelled and as a result find myself fighting many daily battles. I ask You to be my Passover Lamb. Thank You that by accepting Your sacrifice for me and applying Your shed blood to my life, my sins are forgiven. Your angel of death will pass over me so I can know I have eternal life (1 John 5:11)! I invite You to come into my life to live at the center of all I think and do. Amen

REVIEW IT!
God will judge disobedience, but He always provides a way of escape.

god's plan to renew man continues

After man's disobedience and separation from God, God began to provide a way back. He chose Abraham and fulfilled His promise to make him a nation. God gave that nation laws and the blessing of His dwelling in the center of their lives. He provided them something else of great importance—a way to deal with sin.

A. God provided a way back to Him.

    1. After the Israelites were delivered by the Passover Lamb and received God's commandments, what did God say they should do if they sinned unintentionally (see Leviticus 4:1-4)? (According to Hebrews 10:26-27, there is no sacrifice for willful sin.) What would result (see Leviticus 4:20)?

God required a blood sacrifice be made on behalf of the Israelites when they disobeyed the laws He had given. The blood "atoned," or covered, sin so men would be "at-one" with God and have their fellowship with Him restored.

B. God provided the land He promised.

> The Lord made a covenant with Abram, saying, "To your descendants I have given this land, from the river of Egypt as far as the great river, the river Euphrates." (Genesis 15:18)

God said the Israelites should go in and possess the land because He was giving it to them.

    1. What did God, the victorious warrior, promise to do (see Deuteronomy 1:30)?

2. List four reasons the people did not follow God into the land He promised (see Deuteronomy 1:26-27,32).

3. What was the consequence of their disobedience (see Deuteronomy 1:34-36)?

How we struggle with trusting this same mighty God! Like Israel, when things don't look right to us, we may say, "The Lord must hate me." God was giving Israel a blessing beyond anything they could imagine, but in their unbelief and fear they were not willing to receive it. Because they did not trust God to be their victorious warrior, they did not see the Promised Land but instead wandered in the wilderness for forty years until a whole unbelieving generation had died, except for Joshua and Caleb (Numbers 26:65).

4. What did the Lord say the Israelites were to do when they entered the land? What were God's promises to them if they obeyed (see Deuteronomy 6:1-3)?

5. What two things did God warn them not to do (see Deuteronomy 6:10-14)?

6. What did God say would result if they forgot Him and worshiped other gods (see Deuteronomy 6:15)?

Over and over God tells us He is "compassionate and gracious, slow to anger, and abounding in lovingkindness and truth" (Exodus 34:6). However, He is jealous in desiring an exclusive, permanent relationship with us for His honor and our good. Therefore, He is angered when we forget Him and go after other gods. He is a lover who does not want the objects of His affection giving themselves to another.

7. What might cause you to forget the Lord, and what specifically is God asking you to do to ensure that doesn't happen?

The laws of God are not for restraint or bondage. They are for freedom for individual men and for society. Every law of His comes from a heart of love that desires the very best for us — a satisfying life of mental, physical, and spiritual health and a society free from chaos, conflict, and destructive perversions.

LOVE & WAR QUESTION: What does it now mean to you that God is a jealous God?

C. God keeps His promises.

After forty years of leading God's people, Moses died, and God chose Joshua to lead the Israelites into the land of Canaan. This would fulfill the second promise God made to Abraham, that God would give them the land of Canaan.

1. What three things were required of Joshua? What two things would result (see Joshua 1:8)?

2. How does this command with a promise motivate you?

God's idea of prosperity and success may not fit ours. It does not mean financial gain, worldly position, or a stress-free life. However, God's Word does offer us spiritual success as He leads and changes us, removing fear and giving us peace of mind.

How important is the Word of God to you? Do you meditate on it day and night? Do you obey what God asks of you? We see the difficult war between faith and disobedience when Israel was given great promises by God and yet still disobeyed Him.

It took Joshua and the people about twenty-five years to conquer the land, divide it among the twelve tribes, and settle it. But it didn't take long for the people to forget God, who had blessed them with houses they did not build, wells they did not dig, and vineyards they did not plant (Deuteronomy 6:10-15)! Over and over God says, "remember," because He knows we quickly forget.

REVIEW IT!
God is jealous and insists we have no other gods or lovers.

man's (israel's) battle with unfaithfulness continues

God promised to provide a land for His people. Conquering that land was to be all God's doing as He would go ahead of Israel and defeat their enemies. Israel was not to fear but to follow and trust God in order to receive His protection and provision. The Kingdom Books of Joshua through 2 Kings tell of the conquering of the land and of the growth, decline, and eventual destruction of Israel.

A. People with a Short Memory

1. After conquering the land, what did God command Israel to do with the people already living there (see Deuteronomy 7:1-3)?

2. Why did God make such commands (see Deuteronomy 7:4)?

Why would a loving God not allow them to marry the people in the land He gave them and, even worse, command that they destroy those inhabitants? It must be understood that these nations were totally depraved. They were ungodly idol worshipers who practiced temple prostitution and even sacrificed their own children to their false gods! God, being jealous and desiring the best for His people, knew that His children could not cohabitate with evil and not be harmed. They would be tempted to take on their enemies' thinking and eventually become like them. Some enemies cannot be tolerated. They must be totally defeated or wiped out.

LOVE & WAR QUESTION: Is there a habit or practice in your life that needs to be totally annihilated? What is it, and what will you do about it?

3. Before they entered the land, God promised His children blessing for obedience and cursing for disobedience (Deuteronomy 28:1-37). What was the painful consequence God warned the nation they would experience if they were disobedient (see Deuteronomy 28:47-49)?

4. What would be the result of this consequence (see Deuteronomy 28:62-63)?

5. After the Hebrews entered the Promised Land, what did they promise to do (see Joshua 24:24)?

6. What did they do instead (see Judges 10:6)?

7. What did the people substitute for obeying God, their King (see Judges 21:25)?

How often we have good intentions but not the will nor the power to follow through. The people said they would obey God, yet once more they were soon bent on going their own way. And we have the same difficulties or battles in our lives!

B. Israel rejected God as their King.
  1. What did the people eventually demand and why (see 1 Samuel 8:4-5,19-20)?

  2. Who were they rejecting by doing so (see 1 Samuel 8:7)?

Israel was a theocracy. God was their King and a victorious warrior who promised to defeat all their enemies. By demanding a human king to fight their battles, the people were not rejecting Samuel, a judge who ruled over them, but God Himself.

Why do we so quickly forget that God keeps His Word? He does bless obedience, and there are consequences for disobedience. God will not allow us to have other gods, for there are no other gods. He alone is King! He will not allow us to worship that which cannot love, help, or save. After warning that a human king would heavily tax them and even take their children, the people still refused to listen and insisted that their own demands be met (1 Samuel 8:10-19).

 LOVE & WAR QUESTION: What have you learned about man's (your) nature? What can you learn from Israel in regard to why you may be losing life's battles?

The History books show that Israel exchanged their theocracy for a monarchy. The following books show the progression:

- ▶ 1 Samuel: Israel demanded a king. The kingdom was *established*.
- ▶ 2 Samuel: Under King David the twelve tribes were one. The kingdom was *united*.
- ▶ 1 Kings: Though great under Solomon, under his son Rehoboam the kingdom was *divided*.
  - ▪ Jeroboam led a revolt against Solomon's son Rehoboam, and the kingdom was divided.
  - ▪ Jeroboam led the Northern Kingdom of Israel. Rehoboam led the Southern Kingdom of Judah (1 Kings 12).

The Old Testament History books show that God is a gracious Sovereign King who draws us to Himself with love. He longs to bless those who love and obey Him with victory. However, because He is also jealous, just, and holy, He disciplines those who don't obey. Just as disobedience caused the first man and Israel to be separated from God, our disobedience causes us to be exiled, or separated, from Him. Thankfully, God is a King longing to restore and rebuild those far from Him who repent and return. God makes and keeps His promises!

REVIEW IT!
Disobedience always leads to division and separation from God.

god Brings Judgment but promises Renewal

Israel was chosen by God to:

1. Draw other nations to God by demonstrating the blessings of loving and obeying the one true God.
2. Receive the Word of God, write it down, and preserve it.
3. Be the line, or family, through which the Messiah, or Savior, would come.

However, Israel turned from God's love and leading. They followed other nations and worshiped their false gods. If God looked the other way when we sin, He would not be holy and just. But because God is holy and just, He cannot bless disobedience. God is slow to anger, but His wrath is real. God is full of lovingkindness, but He is also a jealous God.

In the History books:

▶ the kingdom was established (1 Samuel)
▶ the kingdom was united (2 Samuel)
▶ the kingdom was divided (1 Kings)
▶ the two kingdoms were exiled (2 Kings)

A. A holy God must judge sin.
   1. Once in the land, what did God have King Solomon build (see 1 Kings 6:1; 7:51)?

   2. What did God then do (see 1 Kings 8:10-11)?

The great God of heaven not only gave His children land "flowing with milk and honey" (Exodus 3:8) but dwelt in their midst in that land as their victorious warrior (Zephaniah 3:17). Though God chose to dwell on earth, heaven and the highest heaven cannot contain Him (1 Kings 8:27). He was their King, but the people did what was "right in [their] own eyes" (Judges 17:6) and chose a human king, though God had warned them to love and serve Him alone.

3. What did the Lord warn would happen if Israel disobeyed (see 1 Kings 9:6-9)?

God warned His children over and over that idolatry (which is spiritual adultery, or unfaithfulness) would result in their exile, or separation, from Him and in the destruction of their land.

LOVE & WAR QUESTION: What idol have you set up in your heart that would make God jealous?

The chief idol over all others is the god of self. Most of our other gods are subservient to this one.

B. God promised not only to judge but also to restore.

Not one word has failed of all His good promise. (1 Kings 8:56)

1. When the Northern Kingdom of Israel served other gods, what happened? (Its capital was Samaria.) (See 2 Kings 17:5-7.)

2. Though they sinned, what did the Lord continue to do (see 2 Kings 17:13)?

3. When the Southern Kingdom of Judah didn't learn from God's exile of Israel and continued to serve other gods, what happened? (Its capital was Jerusalem.) (See 2 Kings 25:8-11.)

Even in our depths of despair God gives promises of hope. We will see how God gave hope through the prophets as He promised the exiles they would return home and rebuild. God truly does want to *renew us in His love*. The Post-Exilic History books of Ezra and Nehemiah tell the history of the three returns of the exiles to rebuild Jerusalem and the temple just as God had promised.

4. What took place that caused the people in exile in Babylon to return to their land (see Ezra 1:1-3)?

5. What did Zerubbabel return to rebuild (see Ezra 3:8; 6:15-16)?

6. What did Ezra return to rebuild (see Ezra 7:10; 10:10-11)?

7. What did Nehemiah return to rebuild (see Nehemiah 2:4-5,17)?

God promised to return the people to the land to restore them, and it happened just as He promised:

▶ Zerubbabel returned to rebuild *the temple*.
▶ Ezra returned to rebuild *the people in God's Word*.
▶ Nehemiah returned to rebuild *the wall of Jerusalem*.

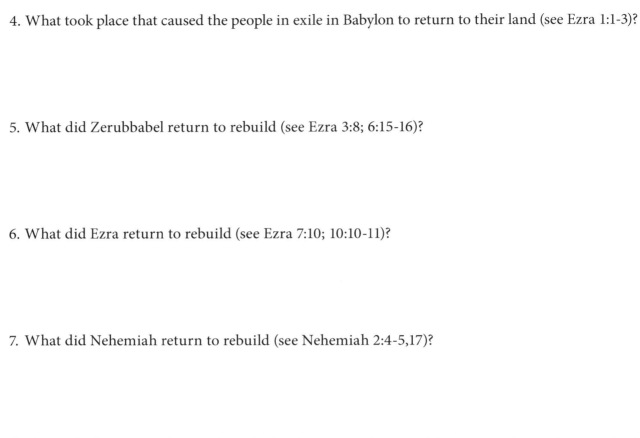

LOVE & WAR QUESTION: How do God's promises to Israel and His purposes for her affect you today?

REVIEW IT!
God invites us to return to Him so He can rebuild and restore our lives.

old testament history

Summary

From the seventeen Old Testament History books we learn about God's love and how our rebellion against Him, which is caused by our sinful nature, forces us to face life's battles separated from Him.

We learn about our Enemy, Satan, and his devious ways. However, we also learn about God, our victorious warrior, and His plan to deliver us.

We see how God invites us to repent, or return to Him, so He can renew us in His love. As we allow Him to live at the center of our lives, He speaks to us, leads us, and rebuilds our relationships with Him and others. This brings Him — and us — great joy!

> The LORD your God is in your midst,
>> A victorious warrior.
>> He will exult over you with joy,
>> He will be quiet in His love (some versions say, "He will renew you in His love"),
>> He will rejoice over you with shouts of joy. (Zephaniah 3:17)

> The LORD, the LORD God, compassionate and gracious, slow to anger, and abounding in lovingkindness and truth. (Exodus 34:6)

▶ The seventeen Old Testament History books show God as our **Sovereign King**.

old testament History
review/Discussion questions

(You may also use the Love & War Questions from your daily homework for discussion or review.)

1. What is the most important thing you learned from your study this week?

2. What has encouraged you the most in the Old Testament History books?

3. What did you discover about God and His ways in the Old Testament History books? How is He revealed as our Sovereign King?

4. What did you learn about yourself and your enemies from this lesson, including from the personal stories?

5. What truth do you need to apply to your life?

#2
old testament writings

god our wisdom

#2 DVD Notes

A Personal Story of
Love and *War*

The Enemy of Death

I love the beach. When I was a child, every summer my family would head to our beach house for a month, which was the highlight of our year. We lived next door to The Crippled Children's Home.

I never liked that name and wanted to rename it "The Children's Play House"; however, very little playing went on there. These children were all confined to wheelchairs.

Every afternoon my mom made us come in from the heat to read and rest. From my bedroom on the second floor I could see the children as they made the long trek down a boardwalk surrounded by sea oats to bathe in the cool salt water. They knew if they could just reach the soothing water of the Gulf, it would bring great relief to their crippled bodies.

They were tenacious. Some had to be carried, and others struggled with heavy, old wooden or metal wheelchairs. The sea oats were so high they couldn't see the water ahead, and I wanted to shout, "Don't give up; you are almost there!" From my upstairs vantage I could see the end of the boardwalk, while they could see only one step ahead, with all the pain that one step brought.

God brought this memory to me as I now walk through breast cancer. He is saying, "Don't give up! Trust Me for each step because I see the end, whereas you can see only one painful step at a time."

One morning after my mastectomy I got out of the shower, bald as a billiard ball and flat on one side with tubes hanging from the other, and I saw myself full-scale in one of those wraparound mirrors! I began to weep. Everything I thought made me feminine was gone, and what remained were scars that would last for life. My husband heard me crying and ran in to find me in a heap. He held me, reassuring me I was beautiful. He said he loved me and was sorry I had to go through this. He was very comforting, but I replied, "Look at me . . . everything is gone, and what about this no hair business?" With that he said, "Honey, you have a really nice head, no lumps or anything!" My tears dissolved into laughter.

I am so grateful that God can see what lies ahead and that He gives strength for each step of the journey. He encourages us to keep on because the end will be worth the effort. I'm also glad He gives us a sense of humor and relationships to help us get to the end with joy. L. B. Cowman wrote, "Joy sometimes needs pain to give it birth."

Today as I painfully trek down this boardwalk of life, I find comfort in the soothing "living water" of God's Word, for He assures me, "His eyes are upon the ways of a man, and He sees all his steps" (Job 34:21) and "In peace I will both lie down and sleep, for You alone, O LORD, make me to dwell in safety" (Psalm 4:8).

Note: The author of this story has since experienced the joy of reaching the end of life and seeing Jesus face-to-face. Because God's Word truly was life to her, she fought the good fight against sickness and death and kept the faith, confident that God can be trusted. She knew He has won the victory and though He does not promise tomorrow, He does promise eternity.

old testament writings

Overview

For the LORD gives wisdom;
> From His mouth come knowledge and understanding.

He stores up sound wisdom for the upright;
> He is a shield to those who walk in integrity. (Proverbs 2:6-7)

▶ These five Old Testament Writing books show God as our **Wisdom**:
Job, Psalms, Proverbs, Ecclesiastes, Song of Solomon

Not only do the Old Testament Writing books give us wisdom to live life, but as in the Personal Story of Love and War you just read, God often uses these books to lead and comfort us in times of suffering and hardship.

The seventeen Old Testament History books we have studied encouraged us by revealing God as our Sovereign King. We can know our life is not without purpose but is under His control. Though He is a sovereign ruler, we saw that He rules with great love because He is gracious, compassionate, and slow to anger and He desires an intimate relationship with us.

However, these books also revealed the harsh consequences of rejecting God's love: separation, conflict, and death. Man's rebellion in the garden brought suffering into the world and caused all our relationships to have difficulties, whether with God or with others. How we need God's wisdom to live a successful life in this fallen world!

The five Old Testament Writings are written in Hebrew poetical form and contain some of the most beautiful and profound words ever written. They have been recorded by the hand of man but come straight from the heart of God. More than simply beautiful words, these books of Wisdom enable us to *walk in integrity* because our King, who is a victorious warrior, will *shield those who walk in His wisdom.*

why did god use poetry?

The Old Testament Writings contain short pithy statements, songs, and poems that help the reader remember a thought or principle. Would you be more likely to remember a person saying, "I love you," or writing you a message such as this?

> The time will come as come it must
> When all the world is dark and still;
> The monuments of man are dust,
> His life an empty void to fill.
>
> Yet in this time of deep despair
> When all the world's torn wide apart,
> I think of thee, how much I care,
> And give to you my soul and heart.

You might have appreciated hearing, "I love you," but years later you would definitely be inclined to remember the poetic words on that piece of paper. Why? Because the message used words less common, yet descriptive and beautiful. Poetry expresses thoughts in uncommon language. It often inspires or challenges, admonishes or encourages, and it is usually memorable.

The chronological relationship of the old testament books

The chart on page 17 shows that the Poetical Books (top of graph) do not add to the history of Israel or advance the chronology. Instead Job was probably written during the time of Abraham and his sons, recorded in the book of Genesis. The majority of the material in the other four Poetical Books was written by King David, a man after God's own heart, and his son King Solomon. King David lived during the time period of 2 Samuel, and Solomon during 1 Kings.

The Old Testament Writings impart wisdom to the reader and are often called "wisdom literature." God gives both wisdom about Himself and wisdom to help us understand ourselves. He shows us how to live with others in peace and love and how to live rightly with God. These wisdom writings help us worship our Sovereign King, and because He is our Wisdom we can fight life's battles and win!

wisdom from job

God is a God of love, but that love is not easy to see in the book of Job. Job suffered immensely. If we suffer does it mean God does not love us?

The book of Job is considered one of the most exquisite pieces of literature ever written. The author is unknown, but scholars have suggested either Moses or Job himself. The book is called a dramatic poem (a story of life or character). It was written during the time of Genesis and reveals much about our Enemy. One of Satan's main goals is to get God's children to doubt His love and power. In the garden he convinced Eve that God's word was not true and could not be trusted. There man lost his first battle.

A. God and Job have a conflict with the Enemy, Satan.

1. What do you learn about Satan (see Job 1:6-7)?

2. Describe what Satan said God had done for Job (see Job 1:8-10).

3. What did Satan propose, and what did God allow (see Job 1:11-12)?

These verses describe an adversary, Satan, with access to heaven and earth but whose actions are limited by a sovereign God. Satan is a fallen angel who rebelled against God and was cast down to the earth. The New Testament calls him "the ruler of this world" (John 12:31) and "the prince of the power of the air" (Ephesians 2:2).

B. Job responded to his suffering.

1. Describe Satan's attack on Job (see Job 1:13-19).

2. What was Job's response to this (see Job 1:20-22)?

3. Since Job did not sin in the midst of this suffering, Satan proposed that if he attacked Job's flesh, Job would curse God (Job 2:4-5). How did God respond to this proposal? What limitation did God place on Satan (see Job 2:6)?

4. Satan smote Job with sore boils from head to toe, and even his wife suggested he curse God and die (Job 2:7-9). What was Job's response? Did Job sin (see Job 2:10)?

LOVE & WAR QUESTION: What additional insight have you received about the ways of your Enemy, Satan?

We clearly see that the reason Job suffered was not because God was angry with him. In fact, God greatly loved Job and was confident in him. Have you ever suffered? Suffering can make God seem far away and even uncaring. Continued suffering often brings depression, hopelessness, and a host of questions: Why, God? Why me? Why now? In the midst of these questions, one thing is certain: When we suffer we need a friend.

C. During his suffering Job's friends failed him.

Job called his friends "worthless physicians" (Job 13:4) and "sorry comforters" (Job 16:2). He said even his relatives failed him and his intimate friends forgot him (Job 19:14).

    1. What did God say was true about Job (see Job 2:3)?

God said Job was blameless, suffering "without cause," yet Job's friends insisted his trouble must be the result of his sin (Job 4:7-8; 32:1-2). Instead of critics, suffering people need a friend to point them to their victorious warrior, who is also their wisdom. What kind of friend are you?

D. Through suffering Job's relationship with God changed.
    1. Job's suffering led him to ask, "If a man dies, will he live again?" (Job 14:14). How did Job answer his own question (see Job 19:25-26)?

Job's suffering went on, and his friends continued to declare him guilty. During these conversations (Job 29–31), Job continued to proclaim his integrity. However, after a season of unexplained suffering he became "I" centered, or self-absorbed. The middle letter of sin and pride is *i*.

    2. During Job's time of questioning, God was silent, but when Job stopped speaking, God began. What are two of the approximately eighty questions God asked Job (see Job 38:4,12)?

After asking Job if he ever created so much as a horse or bird, God asked, "Will you argue with the Almighty? Do you — God's critic — have the answers?" (Job 40:2, TLB). By asking these questions, God was revealing to Job that He alone is sovereign.

    3. God's questions showed Job his own insignificance (Job 40:4). List the ways Job's experience of suffering changed his relationship with God (see Job 42:1-6).

Before his suffering began Job had heard of God, but through his suffering he experienced God personally. There is a vast difference between knowing about God and knowing God. Suffering led Job from self-righteousness to repentance and from mere awareness of God to a more personal relationship with Him.

God did love Job and knew Job loved Him. He had confidence Job would remain upright even through difficult times, and Job did! However, in his suffering, Job became full of "self" (self-pity and self-righteousness). Despite this, God loved Job enough to ask questions to remind him that He — not Job — is sovereign. God created all things and is sovereign over all things, including Satan. God rules!

LOVE & WAR QUESTION: In what ways can suffering change (for the better or the worse) your relationship with God?

The theme of Job appears at first to be man's suffering, but it is really God's sovereignty! Satan tries to use our suffering to cause us to question God's sovereignty and love. Though this book gives wisdom regarding suffering, God may not answer all our questions about why good people suffer. However, in Job's suffering, God showed His greatness. Therefore, we can trust that God is sovereign over all the events in our lives, and we can rest in His everlasting love.

It is important to note that in the end Job yielded to God and prayed for his friends, and the Lord restored Job's fortunes, blessing his latter days more than his earlier ones.

REVIEW IT!
The book of Job gives wisdom to trust that God is sovereign, even in our suffering.

wisdom from psalms

The Psalms reveal the depth of intimacy possible in our love relationship with God. This book of absolute honesty shows us that in any circumstance, we can worship and praise God unashamedly. We can pour out our hearts in praise to our sovereign God, but we can also pour out our anger, fears, doubts, weaknesses, pain, and misery without fear of being rejected, punished, or misunderstood.

A psalm is a lyrical poem (a poem that portrays emotion in the form of a song). Psalms means "that which can be accompanied by instruments." The Psalms composed Israel's hymnbook, teaching us that even our worship is a weapon in our spiritual warfare.

Unlike any other book of the Bible, Psalms is a book of honest emotions and will meet your needs whether you are glad, sad, or mad! For centuries the Psalms have brought healing, help, and hope to people struggling under the difficulties of life. Though praise is difficult in times of hardship, Psalms provides heavenly words that enable us to worship a God of great majesty.

A. The Psalms give healing, help, and hope.
    1. What *comfort* and *hope* do you find in the following?
       a. Psalm 18:1-3

       b. Psalm 55:4-6,16-18

       c. Psalm 68:19

God is everywhere at all times, listening for your cry. He is your comforter and deliverer when the hard times come. He will bear your burdens. What a God!

2. What insights about *forgiveness* and *confession* do you find in the following?
   a. Psalm 32:3-5

   b. Psalm 51:1-4

In these psalms we see that unconfessed sin takes a toll on us physically, mentally and spiritually. However, when we confess (agree with God and turn from sin), God forgives, cleanses, and restores. What a God!

3. What help for *fear, anxiety,* or *depression* do you find in the following?
   a. Psalm 3:3

   b. Psalm 40:1-3

   c. Psalm 46:1-2

God heals and brings joy in the darkest of times. He alone can remove your fears. He will bring you out of a pit, set your feet on a rock, and give you a song. What a good and great God we have!

B. **The Psalms speak of the Word and of worship and praise.**
   1. On the chart on the following page list adjectives that describe what God's Word is and verbs that tell what God's Word does (see Psalm 19:7-8). (*Law, testimony, precepts,* and *commandment* are synonyms for God's Word.)

What God's Word Is	What God's Word Does

2. What other truths do you find about God's Word and what it does?
   a. Psalm 19:10-11

   b. Psalm 119:105

   c. Psalm 119:165

3. List reasons and ways to *worship or praise God*.
   a. Psalm 63:3-4

b. Psalm 145:3-5

LOVE & WAR QUESTION: Summarize what you have learned about God from the Psalms and why, how, and when you should worship Him.

In Job we saw that God is sovereign even in our suffering. The Psalms give wisdom to worship our great God, who is worthy to be praised as Creator, deliverer, and protector.

The wonderful words of the Psalms will draw your eyes upward and away from yourself and your problems and focus them on the greatness of your God, who has all circumstances in your life under His care and control.

 REVIEW IT!
Psalms gives wisdom to worship the mighty God.

wisdom from proverbs

Job and Psalms deal mainly with man's relationship with God, encouraging us to trust and worship Him even in difficult times. Proverbs deals with our relationship not only with God but also with men. It is made up of approximately nine hundred short, practical sayings that give us the wisdom we need to have an intimate relationship with God and healthy, whole, and satisfying relationships with other people. Proverbs is a didactic poem (a poem that appeals to reason and is intended to teach) mostly written by Solomon. It has wisdom or principles for most areas of life: business dealings, finances, marriage, raising children, and so forth.

A. Proverbs gives the source and value of wisdom.

    1. List what you learn about wisdom (skill for living life) from the following:

       a. Proverbs 2:6

       b. Proverbs 3:13

       c. Proverbs 9:10

    Wisdom, or skill for living, comes from God and begins with the fear and knowledge of Him. God's wisdom brings us great blessing when we apply it to our lives.

B. Proverbs gives wisdom for daily living.
   1. List the wisdom for *business or financial dealings* from the following:
     a. Proverbs 3:9-10

     b. Proverbs 11:1

     c. Proverbs 15:27

     d. Proverbs 22:7

God warns of the dangers of borrowing, admonishes us to be honest in our dealings, and requests that we give to Him first.

   2. List wisdom for *marriage* from the following:
     a. Proverbs 5:18-20

     b. Proverbs 14:1

     c. Proverbs 14:11

God exhorts us to be faithful to our mate and to understand that we can destroy our family with our own foolish actions.

3. List wisdom for *raising children* from the following:
    a. Proverbs 13:24

    b. Proverbs 22:6,15

    c. Proverbs 29:15,17

Solomon also wrote, "Because the sentence against an evil deed is not executed quickly, therefore the hearts of the sons of men among them are given fully to do evil" (Ecclesiastes 8:11).

Note that it is important to discipline a child immediately; however, child abuse is a violation of man's laws and God's love. When God speaks of discipline, it is for the purpose of instruction. Parents are to teach, warn, and correct their children as God lovingly teaches, warns, and corrects us. They are to discipline with affection!

4. List wisdom for your *speech* from the following:
    a. Proverbs 12:22

    b. Proverbs 15:1

    c. Proverbs 16:24

d. Proverbs 18:21

Words are powerful either for good or evil. They can build up or tear down. They can heal or hurt. For this reason the New Testament says, "Everyone must be quick to hear, slow to speak and slow to anger" (James 1:19).

LOVE & WAR QUESTION: What specific wisdom has God given you from the Proverbs to enable you to overcome a battle or live skillfully in your home or workplace?

Have you ever done or said something foolish? The wise, timeless truths in the Proverbs were intended to give wisdom for living successfully. However, it has been said, "Reading a Proverb takes only a few seconds; applying a Proverb can take a lifetime."

REVIEW IT!
Proverbs give wisdom for skillful daily living.

wisdom from ecclesiastes

It is believed that King Solomon wrote the Song of Solomon when he was a young man in love, Proverbs when he was middle-aged and full of wisdom, and Ecclesiastes in his later years after he had disobeyed God. Ignoring God's warning, Solomon married foreign women. As God predicted, these wives drew his heart away from God so that he eventually followed after their false gods (1 Kings 11:1-11).

Ecclesiastes is a philosophical book about man's search for a life of meaning or purpose. The natural man living apart from God "says to himself," or reasons in his own mind. He looks "under the sun," or to the material world, for meaning instead of to God.

A. Natural man seeks meaning in life.

1. Where did the author of Ecclesiastes first look for meaning (see Ecclesiastes 1:12-13,16)?

2. What was the result of seeking meaning through human wisdom (see Ecclesiastes 1:17-18)?

3. What was the next way Solomon attempted to find meaning in life? What was the result (see Ecclesiastes 2:1-2)?

4. After looking to pleasure, what did Solomon do to seek meaning in life (see Ecclesiastes 2:4-8)?

5. What was the result of seeking meaning through works or possessions (see Ecclesiastes 2:11)?

6. What impact did the achievement of great works and possessions have on Solomon? Why (see Ecclesiastes 2:17-20)?

7. What is ultimately true about money and possessions (see Ecclesiastes 5:10)?

This philosophical book clearly reminds us that all the things man runs after (money, power, and prestige) bring no lasting satisfaction. Human reasoning and looking to the things of this earth for meaning will always lead to emptiness.

B. Life can be empty, like striving after wind.
   1. What did the writer see as "vanity" (emptiness or meaninglessness) and why (see Ecclesiastes 2:15-16)?

Solomon concluded "all is vanity," or empty, because after all man's work, wealth, wisdom, and striving on earth, he dies and goes to his eternal home. "'Vanity of vanities,' says the Preacher, 'all is vanity!'" (Ecclesiastes 12:5-8).

LOVE & WAR QUESTION: Describe your own life's search for meaning. In what way could this search be described as a battle?

C. The Answer to Having a Full, Meaningful Life

1. What did the writer of Ecclesiastes conclude about life's war (see Ecclesiastes 9:18)?

2. After trying all the world had to offer, what was Solomon's conclusion?

   a. Ecclesiastes 5:7

   b. Ecclesiastes 8:12-13

   c. Ecclesiastes 12:13-14

After trying worldly wisdom, wine, works, wealth, and women, Solomon concluded that life without God is meaningless, and only life with God is meaningful. All is vanity, or emptiness, except to fear God and obey His commandments. Augustine said, "Thou hast created us for Thyself, and our heart is restless till it finds rest in Thee."*

 LOVE & WAR QUESTION: To apply the conclusion of the book of Ecclesiastes to your life, what will you need to do or change?

 REVIEW IT!
Ecclesiastes gives wisdom to live a life of meaning.

---

* A. Norman Jeffares and Martin Gray, *A Dictionary of Quotations* (New York: Barnes and Noble Books, 1997), 31.

wisdom from song of solomon

The Old Testament Writings give us the wisdom we need to live with God and men:

- ▶ **Job** offers wisdom about *God's sovereignty* and trustworthiness even in suffering.
- ▶ **Psalms** gives wisdom to *worship* and praise the great, sovereign God.
- ▶ **Proverbs** gives wisdom to *live a godly life* in an ungodly world.
- ▶ **Ecclesiastes** gives wisdom to *live a life of meaning.*
- ▶ **Song of Solomon** gives wisdom to enjoy the freedom of *marital love.*

Some scholars interpret Song of Solomon as an allegory of God's love for Israel. Others see it as typology, a picture of Christ as the Bridegroom and His church as the bride. When interpreted literally, Song of Solomon is a dramatic poem describing the true beauty of marital love. It is one of the most beautiful love poems ever written, filled with imagery and words of affection and mutual desire.

God is faithful and values faithfulness. However, our contemporary culture devalues faithfulness and insists that sexual immorality is acceptable, exciting, and fun. God, on the other hand, shows that only sex within the context of marriage provides true joy and satisfaction. Sex in marriage should be fulfilling, binding the hearts of husband and wife in a union that God smiles upon with absolute approval. Song of Solomon demonstrates that marital love is a gift from God that is to be enjoyed and that marriage is the most intimate relationship possible between a man and woman.

A. The couple was engaged.

1. How did the future bridegroom describe his fiancée (see Song of Solomon 1:15)?

2. How did the future bride view her fiancé (see Song of Solomon 2:4)?

The future groom reveled in the beauty of his bride-to-be. She felt secure in his love. The groom so respected his beloved that he committed not to arouse her desire for him until the right time (Song of Solomon 2:7; 3:5).

B. The couple married, and the right time arrived.

    1. How did the groom feel on this special day (see Song of Solomon 3:11)?

    2. How did the groom view his new wife (see Song of Solomon 4:7,10)? (You might read 4:1-7 to see how smitten he was.)

The groom described his bride as someone who had waited for him, keeping herself sexually pure (Song of Solomon 4:12). God approved of this couple's exuberant love and desire for one another because they had waited for the right time. His blessing was on them and their marital intimacy, which was His idea from the beginning!

C. The honeymoon was over, and the first marital conflict ensued.

    1. The husband apparently was late getting home, and his wife was already in bed. He called to her, "Open to me, my sister, my darling" (Song of Solomon 5:2). What was her response (see Song of Solomon 5:3)?

"Evidently, Solomon's bride displayed a passive apathy to his late-night advances. We are unaware of the reason for his late arrival, but what often happens in marriage happened here — they just 'missed' each other. He had a certain expectation, but she responded indifferently. Who was in the wrong? Maybe both of them. But regardless, they found themselves in a marital predicament. So he left and went back to work."*

    2. The husband left, and his wife didn't respond to him in time. What happened next (see Song of Solomon 5:4,6)?

---

* Big Dream Ministries, Inc., *The Amazing Collection: The Poetical Books* (Alpharetta, GA: Big Dream Ministries, Inc., 2004), 132.

3. After their conflict, how did the wife describe her husband (see Song of Solomon 5:16)? (Song of Solomon 5:10-16 shows how smitten she was.)

4. How did the husband describe his feelings toward his wife (see Song of Solomon 7:6-8)?

We can learn from this couple's willingness to forgive and restore their relationship. Even after conflict, their desire for one another was not any less intense than before. Rather than take the other for granted, they valued each other. They chose to praise their mate's positive traits rather than dwell on their negatives.

D. The conflict was resolved.

1. What did the wife propose to restore intimacy with her husband (see Song of Solomon 7:10-12)?

2. What do we learn about love in marriage from Song of Solomon 8:6-7?

Song of Solomon celebrates romantic, sexual, erotic, passionate love in marriage. A man and his wife are to enjoy one another and love one another all the days of their lives. They are to realize that true love cannot be bought or quenched.

LOVE & WAR QUESTION: What specific wisdom have you received about marriage from Song of Solomon?

 **REVIEW IT!**
Song of Solomon gives wisdom to enjoy the freedom of marital love.

old testament writings (poetry)

Summary

> For the LORD gives *wisdom*;
>> From His mouth come knowledge and understanding.
> He stores up sound wisdom for the upright;
>> He is a shield to those who walk in *integrity*. (Proverbs 2:6-7, emphasis added)

The five Old Testament Writings give wisdom for every area of life. They provide God's wisdom in our war with forces bent on destroying all of our relationships. As the proverb above states, when we obey God's words of wisdom, we will *walk in integrity*. God then becomes a *shield* of protection for us. Therefore, application of these truths will guard or heal all of our relationships.

The Old Testament Writings show us the depth of God's love for us. He is:

▶ the sovereign God in our suffering (Job)
▶ the God of comfort to be worshiped (Psalms)
▶ the giver of wise counsel for daily living (Proverbs)
▶ the source of a life of meaning (Ecclesiastes)
▶ the giver of joy and freedom in marital love (Song of Solomon)

We desire love, but war is unavoidable; however, in both our search for love and in our inevitable wars, God has provided abundantly for us!

▶ The five Old Testament Writing books show God as our **Wisdom**.

old Testament writings (poetry)
Review/Discussion Questions

(You may also use the Love & War Questions from your daily homework for discussion or review.)

1. What specific wisdom did God give in one or more of the following areas that is most helpful in your life today? Give a specific example of how that wisdom is being lived out.
   ▶ Suffering
   ▶ Worship of God
   ▶ Relationships
   ▶ Meaning of life
   ▶ Marriage

2. What is the most important thing you learned about God in the Old Testament Writing books?

3. What is the most important thing you learned about yourself and your battles?

4. What is wisdom and how do you get it?

5. What did you learn from the personal stories?

#3
old testament prophecy

god our judge

#3 DVD Notes

A Personal Story of
Love and *War*

THE ENEMY OF DIVORCE

When I was five years old my mother shared with me the forgiveness of Jesus, and I knelt by my bed and received Him as my Savior. However, as a teenage jock my life wasn't always that godly. I was tormented by my sin and would ask Jesus to come into my life again and again. There came a day when I had to stop calling God a liar by not believing He was in my life. I had to believe that I was forgiven in spite of my struggles and that what I needed was to surrender my life to His will.

However, in my twenties I met a pretty party girl. She was definitely my choice for a wife, but not God's choice. Because of my principles and values I had saved my sex life for marriage, and I married believing it was forever. As many young couples do, we had the normal problems of getting to know one another and adjusting to our differences, but life was good. She then began to model and come in late at night. She always had an excuse, but I wanted her with me.

As a salesman I spent much time on the road, but the highlight of my week was coming home. One Monday I left on a week-long trip across the country and was scheduled to come home on Friday; however, I finished my business a day early and was excited at the prospect of going home to surprise my wife because I had really missed her. When I arrived home unannounced, my best friend's car was in the driveway. Since he and his wife had just given birth to a baby boy, I thought they must be visiting. I went into the house and, with the exception of music playing, all was quiet. I took my luggage to the bedroom and upon opening the door found my wife with the person I thought was my best friend. I was speechless and felt doubly betrayed.

Because I sold items of great value I was licensed to carry a gun and, in fact, had a loaded one. In my hurt, I ordered them both out of the house without any clothes and no identification. They left with the keys to his car, cursing me all the way out the door. She moved in with him the next day (into one of our rental properties) and sued me for divorce. To compound the betrayal, the divorce papers accused me of unfaithfulness!

For two years I tried my best to save the marriage. I didn't want her the way she was but the way I knew she could be. At the final hearing the judge asked if the marriage could be saved. I answered, "Yes, anything is possible with God." He then turned to my wife and asked if the marriage could be saved. She said, "#@*% no!" After twelve years together, the gavel came down and a judge declared that my marriage was over.

Divorce is a very difficult thing. I felt excruciating pain. In marriage two people are "superglued" together, and divorce is like ripping two bonded things apart. There is irreparable damage. Through it all God gave me peace not to worry about the lies or the outcome.

Because I wouldn't want to marry a promiscuous woman, I didn't want to be an immoral man. Once more I begged God for the strength to put my sex drive on the back burner until he brought the perfect wife. Although years have passed and I am still unmarried, God has granted me that strength to this day.

We can say a prayer for salvation, but the evidence of that salvation is a changed life. My life today is not sinless, but I do sin less because I want to please my Savior. He has provided an intimate relationship with Him and wonderful friendships to fill the human void. When God says we are to "believe" in Jesus, it means to "adhere to, trust in, and rely on Him." I know I can "adhere to Jesus" and never fear being torn apart from Him!

old testament prophecy

Overview

For the LORD is our judge,
  The LORD is our lawgiver,
  The LORD is our king;
  He will save us. (Isaiah 33:22)

▶ These seventeen books of Old Testament Prophecy show God as our **Judge**:

  ▶ *Major Prophets:* Isaiah, Jeremiah, Lamentations, Ezekiel, Daniel
  ▶ *Early Minor Prophets:* Hosea, Joel, Amos, Obadiah, Jonah, Micah
  ▶ *Later Minor Prophets:* Nahum, Habakkuk, Zephaniah, Haggai, Zechariah, Malachi

God is jealous and desires an exclusive, permanent relationship with those He loves. He understands the pain of a betrayed husband because like the wife in the personal story "The Enemy of Divorce," God's bride, Israel, ran after other lovers. Through the Old Testament prophets God pleaded with Israel to return to the safety of His love.

The prophetic books contain some of God's most poignant words of love — words like, "I will betroth you to Me forever . . . in lovingkindness and in compassion" (Hosea 2:19). Through these books God not only pleaded with Israel to return to Him but also warned her of the dangers of straying and playing the harlot.

Each prophet voiced both warning and hope. Isaiah warned, "The LORD is our judge"; however, he also gave hope: "The LORD is our king; He will save us" (Isaiah 33:22). When we think of a judge we certainly don't imagine a lover but someone stern and perhaps condemning. However, our judge has already described Himself as full of lovingkindness and compassion, gracious and slow to anger. He is a different kind of judge, one who judges with love, justice, and mercy.

We have seen that the Old Testament can be divided into three sections:

  ▶ The _____ Old Testament _____ books reveal God as our _____.

  ▶ The _____ Old Testament _____ books reveal God as our _____.

  ▶ The *seventeen* Old Testament *Prophecy* books reveal God as our **Judge**.

The Chronological Relationship of the Old Testament Books chart on page 17 shows that the prophets *do not advance the chronological story* of the Old Testament history that ended with the book of Nehemiah.

The majority of the Old Testament prophecies were written during the time period of 2 Kings. At that time the kingdom was divided because Rehoboam, Solomon's son, did not reign with wisdom. Instead of listening to wise counsel to lighten the hard service required of the people, he listened to his peers who suggested he add to their load. Therefore, the people revolted and the kingdom was divided, with Jeroboam as the northern king and Rehoboam as the southern king. In the ensuing years, the Northern Kingdom of Israel had nineteen kings, all of whom were wicked. The Southern Kingdom of Judah had twenty kings, and only eight were good. All together, thirty-nine kings rejected or despised God's Word, which led to the worship of other gods. Unfortunately, as the leader goes, so go the people.

The **Keeping the Prophets in Perspective** chart on page 76 shows when and to whom the prophetic messages were given. The first five prophetical books (Isaiah — Daniel) were written to Judah and are called Major Prophets, not because they are more important, but because they are longer in length. The last twelve called Minor Prophets (Hosea — Malachi) are shorter in length and were written to various nations.

In the Old Testament we've seen God's great love for all people revealed in several ways:

1. **God always warns before He judges.**
   With individuals in the Garden of Eden and with the nation of Israel, God warned of the consequences of disobedience. In both cases He warned that rebellion would lead to separation from Him. Sin in the garden would lead to separation and to death. The rebellion of Israel would lead to separation through exile. Through the prophets he warned other nations as well.

2. **God always provides a place of spiritual safety when judgment comes.**
   He provided the ark for Noah and the Passover lamb for the nation of Israel. However, men had to get in the ark and apply the blood of the lamb.

3. **God always provides a way back to Him.**
   After men sinned and were separated from God, He provided a blood sacrifice to atone for sin. Even before the exile, God provided a promise that He would bring rebellious Israel back to the land and restore His relationship with them.

All the prophets have important messages for today. The New Testament says, "You too be patient; strengthen your hearts, *for the coming of the Lord is near.* Do not complain, brethren, against one another, so that you yourselves may not be judged; behold, *the Judge* is standing right at the door. As an example, brethren, of suffering and patience, take *the prophets* who spoke in the name of the Lord" (James 5:8-10, emphasis added).

The prophets reveal God as our Judge. Since "the Judge is standing right at the door," we need to pay attention to "the prophets who spoke in the name of the Lord" and are "an example . . . of suffering and patience" while giving the unpopular message that a just Judge cannot overlook sin. "The coming of the Lord is near," so get right with your Judge!

	ISRAEL	JUDAH	EXILE IN BABYLONIA / POST-EXILE JERUSALEM	ASSYRIA	EDOM
800 BC		JOEL 835 BC			OBADIAH 848 BC
700 BC	AMOS 760 BC HOSEA 755 BC	ISAIAH 740 BC MICAH 735 BC		JONAH 793 BC	
722 BC	ISRAEL IS CONQUERED BY ASSYRIA				
600 BC		JEREMIAH 627 BC ZEPHANIAH 632 BC HABAKKUK 609 BC	EZEKIEL 592 BC DANIEL 605 BC	NAHUM 664 BC	
586 BC	JUDAH IS EXILED TO BABYLON				
500 BC		LAMENTATIONS 586 BC	HAGGAI 520 BC ZECHARIAH 520 BC		
400 BC			MALACHI 432 BC		
400 BC / 0 BC	400 SILENT YEARS				

JESUS CHRIST THE MESSIAH IS BORN

god sent men called prophets

Prophets, or "seers" (1 Samuel 9:9), were men chosen by God to speak in place of God. (The letters *p-r-o* in the word *prophet* mean "in place of.") God called prophets and spoke to them in visions and dreams (Isaiah 1:1; Daniel 7:1) or face-to-face (Deuteronomy 34:10; 18:15-18). The prophets then told the people what God had said. Prophets would either "tell forth" a message from God or "foretell" the future.

A. God's Purposes for the Prophets

> Surely the LORD God does nothing
>> Unless He reveals His secret counsel
>> To His servants the prophets. (Amos 3:7)

1. Through the prophets, what did God instruct His people to do (see 2 Kings 17:13)?

After men rejected God's love, bringing judgment upon themselves, God sent prophets to *warn* them. Daniel said prophets *speak in God's name* and *teach* His words (Daniel 9:6,10). Through prophets God would reveal His plan for the future and teach men how to live in light of that plan.

2. List the downward spiral of the people's response and actions to the prophets' warnings (see 2 Kings 17:14-17).

When Israel ignored God's messages and began to live apart from His laws, they eventually became as cruel and perverted as the neighboring nations, even sacrificing their own children to false gods.

B. God sent prophets to warn and teach His people.

The people were religious. They were *sacrificing and praying*, but they had other gods (Isaiah 1:11-15; 2:8). It is hard to see our sin when we are religious. Religious people may go to church, practice rituals, and try hard to be good. However, they may have the gods of *self-effort, self-reliance*, and *self-righteousness* or perhaps the gods of *possessions, people*, and *position*. The prophets tell us about sin because religious people must see their need for God.

1. What are two consequences of our sin (see Isaiah 59:2)?

2. Why does man sin (see Jeremiah 17:9)?

3. In spite of our deceitful heart, what did God promise about His love (see Jeremiah 31:3)?

God's prophetic messages came from His heart of love for His people. In addition to the prophets who wrote the seventeen prophetic books, the Old Testament speaks of many other prophets. These include Gad (1 Samuel 22:5), Nathan (2 Samuel 7:2), Jehu (1 Kings 16:7), Elijah (1 Kings 18:36), Elisha (1 Kings 19:16), Shemaiah (2 Chronicles 12:5), Iddo (2 Chronicles 13:22), Hanani (2 Chronicles 16:7), and Oded (2 Chronicles 28:9).

God sent these prophets because as a just judge, He must judge our sin, but as a loving judge, He wants to spare us. Love is patient; therefore, God gave the people many opportunities to repent and return to Him. The prophet Joel said, "Whoever calls on the name of the Lord will be delivered" (2:32).

 LOVE & WAR QUESTION: Summarize the role of a prophet and explain why God sent so many. What does this say to you personally?

C. Satan counterfeits God's prophets.

Anytime God gives something real, Satan counterfeits it. A prophet's message frees men from sin, but Satan tries to keep us in bondage. God says a true prophet is accurate 100 percent of the time (Deuteronomy 18:22). The husband of a modern fortune-teller said, "My wife has a gift — she is accurate 80 percent of the time." According to God's test, she is not a true prophet!

1. How does Deuteronomy 13:1-3 challenge you to be a student of God's Word?

2. According to Deuteronomy 13:5, death was the punishment for prophets who did what?

Today, we would be greatly impressed with anyone who performs miracles, but God says even great wonders are not a sign of a true prophet. How will you discern a true prophet? The true prophet's teachings will cause you to follow and serve the one true God. It is impossible to know if someone is teaching against the Word of God unless we know what that Word says!

3. Instead of God's truth, what kinds of messages did the people want to hear from the prophets (see Isaiah 30:9-11)?

4. What three things did God say were "appalling and horrible" (see Jeremiah 5:30-31)?

5. What do we learn about true and false prophets (see Jeremiah 23:16,21-22)?

LOVE & WAR
QUESTION: How will you identify or discern a false prophet today?

True prophets encourage people to return to God and reject evil. God gave true prophets, but the people were constantly tempted to listen to false ones because their message was more pleasant than truth. The same is true today! We need to know the truth of God's Word so we will not be deceived by false teaching.

 REVIEW IT!
Our judge exults over us with truth and love, while false prophets offer lies.

The five major prophets

(ISAIAH, JEREMIAH, LAMENTATIONS, EZEKIEL, DANIEL)

There are five Major Prophets, or longer prophetic books. The **Keeping the Prophets in Perspective** chart on page 76 shows that Isaiah and Jeremiah wrote *before the exile* of Judah. They warned of her coming fate. Ezekiel and Daniel wrote *during the exile* to encourage the people who were scattered. All the prophets gave warnings, but they never warned without also giving hope.

A. God's Message of Warning and Hope Through *Isaiah*

1. Isaiah was written before either the Northern or Southern Kingdom was exiled. What did God warn through Isaiah? (see Isaiah 42:8)?

2. Because of their idolatry, the people were eventually exiled from their land. However, in His grace God said He would call a man to return the exiles and rebuild Jerusalem and the temple. What was that man's name (see Isaiah 44:28)?

3. What reason did God give Cyrus for the fact that He would use him to return His people to their land (see Isaiah 45:6-7)?

God gave Isaiah this prophecy 150 years before Cyrus was born! Through the Old Testament Prophets we see that God knows and controls all things, including the future. Ezra 1:1-3 shows that God "stirred up the spirit of Cyrus" to return the people.

4. What hope did God give regarding war in a future day (see Isaiah 2:4)?

B. God's Message of Warning and Hope Through *Jeremiah*

    1. Unfaithful Israel loved other gods. Jeremiah wrote after the Northern Kingdom of Israel was exiled to warn the Southern Kingdom of Judah to avoid the same judgment. What did God say about Israel and His relationship with her (see Jeremiah 3:6-8)?

    2. Since Judah also was unfaithful, what specifically did God warn her (see Jeremiah 25:10-11)?

    3. What promise of hope did God give through Jeremiah (see Jeremiah 29:1,10)?

    4. Why would God restore Israel (see Jeremiah 29:11)?

Wow! That is love! Even in their disobedience God had a plan for their welfare, to give them a future and a hope. After every rebellion God has always provided man a way back to Him.

C. God's Message of Warning and Hope Through Jeremiah in *Lamentations*

    1. Jeremiah wrote Lamentations to lament the destruction of Jerusalem after Judah refused to listen to God's warnings. Describe how God's judgment feels (see Lamentations 3:16-18).

    2. What brought Jeremiah renewed hope (see Lamentations 3:21-24)?

D. God's Message of Warning and Hope Through *Ezekiel*

   1. What did God say to the prophet Ezekiel to motivate him to warn God's people (see Ezekiel 3:17-19)?

   2. Many scholars believe Ezekiel 28:11-17 goes beyond describing a human king and actually refers to Satan. If this is true, what do you learn about him?

   3. While the people were in exile, God gave Ezekiel two visions. First he saw the glory of the Lord leave the temple as the judgment for Judah's rebellion. Then he saw the glory of the Lord return. What additional hope did God give for the future (see Ezekiel 36:24-27)?

Though God would leave, He promised to return. God gave greater hope by promising that when His people repent and return to Him, He will put His Spirit in them to cause them to walk in His ways. The Holy Spirit does the same for us!

LOVE & WAR QUESTION: As you understand it, what was the war the prophets warned about?

E. God's Message of Warning and Hope Through *Daniel*

   1. As the people neared the end of seventy years in exile, Daniel read God's prophecy through Jeremiah that after seventy years they would return to the land. What did this foreknowledge cause Daniel to do (see Daniel 9:2-4)?

2. List the reasons Daniel gave for their exile and Jerusalem's destruction (see Daniel 9:5-6).

3. What warning along with hope did God give Daniel for a future day (see Daniel 12:1-2)?

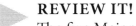

LOVE & WAR QUESTION: What is one encouraging truth in the Major Prophets that gives hope to your life?

> **REVIEW IT!**
> The five Major Prophets warn that God will not give His glory to another.

the six early minor prophets

(Hosea, Joel, Amos, Obadiah, Jonah, Micah)

God does not want to punish people, but He is a just God. The Early Minor Prophets are called early because they wrote *before either the Northern or Southern Kingdom of Israel was exiled.* They are called minor because they are *shorter in length.*

As you can see from the **Keeping the Prophets in Perspective** chart on page 76, most of the prophets wrote to the Southern Kingdom of Judah, but two of the Early Minor Prophets, Hosea and Amos, wrote to the Northern Kingdom of Israel before their exile to warn them to return to God. The prophets' messages included both warnings regarding the people's sin and hope if they would repent.

A. God's Message of Warning and Hope Through *Hosea*

1. Hosea the prophet was hurt by an unfaithful wife. God also had an unfaithful wife, yet what words of love did God proclaim to His bride, Israel (see Hosea 2:19-20)?

2. What did God ask His people to do? What would be the result if they obeyed (see Hosea 14:1,4)?

B. God's Message of Warning and Hope Through *Joel*

1. God warned that Judah's disobedience would bring devastation like a recent plague of swarming locusts. For God to allow an enemy nation to destroy Judah does not seem loving. Yet God gave ample opportunity to avoid this judgment. What did He beg Judah to do and why (see Joel 2:12-13)?

2. What did God then promise His people (see Joel 2:25-26)?

C. God's Message of Warning and Hope Through *Amos*

    1. Amos saw God with a plumb line showing that Israel was out of line and deserving of divine judgment. What did Amos say the people would experience (see Amos 8:11)?

    2. What future promise did God give through Amos to provide hope to His people (see Amos 9:14-15)?

D. God's Message of Warning and Hope Through *Obadiah*

    1. In His love, God sent prophets to warn eighteen different nations, including enemies of His people such as Edom. What was their sin and how would God judge them (see Obadiah 1:3-4)?

    2. What specific warning did God give Edom (the house of Esau) (see Obadiah 1:18)?

Because the Edomites refused to listen to God's warning and mistreated their brother nation Israel, no hope was given. Petra, the city of Edom, lies in ruins to this day, partially fulfilling God's prophetic Word!

E. God's Message of Warning and Hope Through *Jonah*

1. Assyria was another enemy nation that received a warning from God. God asked Jonah to go east to warn Assyria that their wickedness had come before God. However, Jonah went west instead! Jonah knew the Assyrians were cruel. They tortured their captives by skinning or impaling them. He also knew God was compassionate and loving (Jonah 4:1-2). How did God get the prophet Jonah's attention (see Jonah 1:17; 2:1,10)?

2. What was God's message to Assyria? What was their response (see Jonah 3:4-5,8)?

3. How did God respond to their repentance (see Jonah 3:10)?

God finally got Jonah's attention, and Jonah went to Assyria to warn the people there. The Assyrians repented, and God did not judge them. Soon the Assyrians would forget God, and God would use them to judge Israel. However, because of their earlier heart change, the Assyrians were less cruel when they captured Israel. Therefore, by sending prophets, God was showing love not only to Israel's enemies but to His own people as well.

F. God's Message of Warning and Hope Through *Micah*

1. Through Micah, God indicted leaders, priests, and prophets. What were they doing wrong? What would be the consequences (see Micah 3:11-12)?

2. How would God's love affect His anger toward the people's sin? What does God do with our sins (see Micah 7:18-19)?

When we repent, God, in His love, casts our sins into the depths of the sea. They are buried . . . gone! As Corrie ten Boom has said, "I believe God then places a sign out there that says, NO FISHING ALLOWED."*

LOVE & WAR QUESTION: What did you learn about God, His ways, and His judgments through the Early Minor Prophets?

REVIEW IT!
God's prophets warned but followed their warnings with hope.

---

* Corrie ten Boom, *Tramp for the Lord* (Christian Literature Crusade and Revell, 1974).

the six later minor prophets

(NAHUM, HABAKKUK, ZEPHANIAH, HAGGAI, ZECHARIAH, MALACHI)

The **Keeping the Prophets in Perspective** chart on page 76 shows that the last six prophets are called later because they wrote *after the Northern Kingdom of Israel was exiled* to Assyria in 722 BC. They are called minor because they are *shorter in length*. Since Israel had already been exiled and scattered, two of the Later Prophets wrote to Judah, the Southern Kingdom, to warn them to repent and be spared a similar fate. Judah did not listen and was exiled to Babylon in 586 BC.

A. God's Message of Warning and Hope Through *Nahum*

1. After God sent Jonah to warn Israel's enemy, Assyria, they repented momentarily but eventually went back to their old ways. About 130 years later God sent Nahum to warn Assyria that because of their disobedience, judgment was imminent. What do we learn about God (see Nahum 1:2-3)?

2. What hope did Nahum give (see Nahum 1:7)?

B. God's Message of Warning and Hope Through *Habakkuk*

1. The Northern Kingdom had been exiled. Habakkuk saw great wickedness in the Southern Kingdom as well, and his faith wavered. Habakkuk asked God why He was not doing something about Judah's sin. What was God's response (see Habakkuk 1:5-6)?

2. God's answer was that He was doing something. He was sending the fierce Chaldeans, or Babylonians! This was not the answer Habakkuk wanted; however, as he waited for the coming attack of the Babylonians, what did Habakkuk do and why (see Habakkuk 3:18-19)?

C. God's Message of Warning and Hope Through *Zephaniah*

1. Zephaniah spoke about "the day of the LORD." List what you learn about that future day (see Zephaniah 1:14-15,18).

2. What hope did Zephaniah give regarding that day (see Zephaniah 3:16-17)?

D. God's Message of Warning and Hope Through *Haggai*

1. The exiles of Judah returned to their land from Babylon and started to rebuild the temple, but then they got distracted building their own houses. What did God say through Haggai (see Haggai 1:7-8)?

2. How did the people respond to God's message (see Haggai 1:12)?

We see a loving God who wanted the temple rebuilt so He could live in the midst of His people once more. If you have gone astray, God wants you to return to Him. He will dwell in you and rebuild your life as well.

E. God's Message of Warning and Hope Through *Zechariah*

   1. Like Haggai, Zechariah also encouraged the exiles to finish rebuilding the temple, but there was opposition. What is one way Satan, our Enemy, attacks (see Zechariah 3:1)?

   2. How is Satan defeated and all our battles won (see Zechariah 3:2; 4:6)?

LOVE & WAR QUESTION: What other insights about your enemies and your daily wars have you gotten from the prophets?

F. God's Message of Warning and Hope Through *Malachi*

   1. God gave His last prophetic message before four hundred years of silence, during which time He sent no prophets. What was one of God's last warnings regarding His coming (see Malachi 3:5-6)?

   2. What was one of God's last Old Testament promises (see Malachi 3:1)?

LOVE & WAR QUESTION: Is there a famine in your life for the Word of God? What have the prophets said to you about the importance of God's Word?

 REVIEW IT!
In His love God sent many prophets to warn and to teach.

the prophets, jesus, and you

The prophets wrote hundreds of years before Christ came to earth, yet they still speak to us today. Soon after Jesus' resurrection He spoke about the prophets: "'O foolish men and slow of heart to believe in *all that the prophets have spoken!*' . . . Then beginning with Moses and with *all the prophets*, He explained to them the things concerning Himself in *all the Scriptures*. . . . 'All things which are written about Me in the Law of Moses and *the Prophets* and the Psalms must be fulfilled'" (Luke 24:25,27,44, emphasis added).

Jesus affirmed that the entire Old Testament speaks about Him! He included in His claim the books of Moses, generally agreed to be the first five History books; the Psalms, which is a Writing book; and all the Prophets. He said we are foolish if we don't know and believe these books! Yet for many of us, the prophetic books are clean, untouched pages in our Bibles. All the Prophets are important for us today because they not only warn us but also foretell the future.

A. Over three hundred Old Testament prophecies regarding the Messiah were fulfilled at Jesus' first coming.

    1. What did the prophets say would be unique about the Messiah's birth?

       a. Isaiah 7:14

       b. Isaiah 9:6-7

    2. Where did a prophet foretell an eternal ruler would be born (see Micah 5:2)?

3. Though a king, what would the Messiah ride into Jerusalem (see Zechariah 9:9)?

4. The prophets foretold Jesus' birth. What did they say about His death?
   a. Isaiah 50:6

   b. Isaiah 53:5-6

   c. Isaiah 53:7

   d. Isaiah 53:9

B. **Over four hundred Old Testament prophecies have not yet been fulfilled but will be when Jesus returns.**
   1. What did the prophet Zechariah say will happen when Jesus returns (see Zechariah 14:4,9)?

   2. What will happen when Jesus reigns on earth (see Isaiah 11:6,9)?

   3. What will be included in the judgment when Jesus comes (see Isaiah 24:19-21,23)?

4. What blessings will result when Jesus comes (see Isaiah 25:8-9)?

5. What will happen after Jesus judges the earth (see Isaiah 65:17)?

6. What will Jesus do for Israel when He returns (see Jeremiah 23:5-6)?

7. What else will be true when Christ reigns (see Micah 4:3)?

These things have not yet happened, but they will! God said it and you can count on it because love never fails.

 LOVE & WAR QUESTION: What is the most important thing you have learned from the prophets about God, your Judge?

 **REVIEW IT!**
God gives hope that after judgment He will return to restore and reign!

old testament prophecy

Summary

The seventeen books of Old Testament Prophecy show how God loved His people enough to send many prophets to warn that disobedience would bring judgment and defeat.

The prophets warned both the Northern and Southern Kingdoms (and even enemy nations) to get right with God. The prophets also warn us today about His coming judgment. However God never warns without also giving hope.

To find the love we desire and win the daily wars we face, we must know that God is our *Sovereign King*, our *Wisdom*, and our *Judge*.

Only a very loving judge would:

1. Warn us that sin will separate us from the presence of our Protector.
2. Send warnings before He sends correction.
3. Provide a place of safety when judgment comes.
4. Provide a way back to Him.
5. Promise restoration.

> For the LORD is our judge [warning],
>> The LORD is our lawgiver,
>> The LORD is our king;
>> He will save us [hope]. (Isaiah 33:22)

▶ The seventeen books of Old Testament Prophecy reveal God as our **Judge**.

old Testament prophecy
Review/Discussion Questions

(You may also use the Love & War Questions from your daily homework for discussion or review.)

1. What did God say to you through the Personal Stories of Love and War?

2. What did you learn about God and the prophets?

3. What did you learn about false prophets?

4. What is the most important thing for you personally from the seventeen books of Old Testament Prophecy?

5. Why do we need to understand the Old Testament prophets today?

#4

New Testament History

✝

Jesus our savior

#4 DVD Notes

A Personal Story of
Love and *War*

The Enemy of Self

My mother recalls that the first words out of my mouth were, "I'd rather do it myself." For years, self-effort was my approach to life and religion. Jesus (the living Word) and the Bible (His written Word) simply had no place in my life.

However, when I was twenty-six years old, someone asked, "If you died right now, do you have assurance you would go to heaven?" I had no such assurance, but trusting my self-righteousness, I responded, "I haven't done any of the biggies; I've never murdered anyone or robbed a bank. And I have pins to prove I didn't miss church once for twelve years in a row. I have spent my life trying to get my good deeds to outweigh my bad."

The person who asked me this question explained, "God does not have a scale, but His standard is perfection. The Bible says God is too pure to look on sin; therefore, only perfect people would be in heaven." I knew that standard of perfection left me out! She said, "God's Word also says we all have sinned and the wage, or payment, for sin is death. That is bad news, but the good news is Jesus lived a perfect life and had no sin of His own to die for; therefore, He could choose to die to pay for ours!" A light came on. At that moment I received Jesus into my life, and my *Judge* became my *Savior*! I understood I needed Jesus *to face death*.

Eight months later I realized I needed Jesus *to face life*. My infant son was born five weeks premature with a severe birth defect. He was three and a half pounds and sixteen inches long, and his stomach and intestinal tract were outside his body. The doctors predicted he would die, and I was powerless to fix him. Even worse, I reasoned God must be punishing me for my sins, so my baby's condition must be my fault. What a heavy load of guilt to bear. I desperately needed God's *Wisdom*!

I had often prayed. Actually, I made deals with God: "You do this for me, and I'll do something nice for You." But now I needed to know if my baby's condition was a result of my sin. For the first time I allowed God to talk back. There was always a Bible on my nightstand, but it seemed irrelevant — who cares who begat whom? I now picked up that Bible and read in John 9 about Jesus walking with His disciples and seeing a beggar who had been blind since birth. The disciples asked Jesus, "Who sinned, this man or his parents, that he would be born blind?" (verse 2). Jesus said he was born blind for no man's sins but to show the power of God (verse 3)! What a relief! God wasn't punishing me; He wanted to show His power . . . and He did. My baby boy survived nine surgeries and now has two sons of his own!

I was learning that God truly is the *Sovereign King* with power to heal and to forgive. Through the Prophets I realized that God buries our sin in the sea so we can't see it (Micah 7:19) and puts our sin behind His back so He can't see it (Isaiah 38:17)! The load of my guilt was gone!

Anyone who honestly looks at the plan of God throughout the Bible and examines the claims of Jesus will never be the same because the Sovereign King became Immanuel, God with us. Through birth defects, job loss, sickness, betrayal, and death, God has made clear to me that we need both the *death* and the *life* of Jesus Christ. *Jesus' death* provides forgiveness of sin and the promise of heaven when we die. *Jesus' life* provides strength and wisdom while we live. This truly is good news!

New Testament History

Overview

Greater love has no one than this, that one lay down his life for his friends. (John 15:13)

▶ These five New Testament History books show Jesus as our **Savior**:
Matthew, Mark, Luke, John, Acts

The personal story "The Enemy of Self" shows that God, our Savior, wants to fight and win the battles we have with guilt and life's difficulties. Unfortunately, when we choose to live apart from God, we choose to fight these battles on our own. The New Testament History books reveal that we need both the death of Jesus and the life of Jesus (the Holy Spirit) to conquer our guilt and fears. We see the love of God in His coming as Immanuel, God with us. God came to die for us, and there is no greater love than to lay down your life for another.

Since our days in the garden, man has sought love and found war. War with God and man was a high price to pay for rejecting God's love, but all men who have been born into this world have found conflict, pain, and death to be inevitable. Satan is our Enemy without, and sin is our enemy within. Satan's great sin (and ours) is the desire to live independently from God.

For several thousand years God promised a seed of Abraham who would crush Satan's head, though His own heel would be bruised in the process (Genesis 3:15). God pointed to a Passover lamb whose blood would protect men from death if they were willing to personally apply it. What God promises He does provide.

▶ The _____ Old Testament _____ books reveal God as our _____.

▶ The _____ Old Testament _____ books reveal God as our _____.

▶ The _____ Old Testament _____ books reveal God as our _____.

▶ The _five_ New Testament _History_ books reveal Jesus as our **Savior**.

The **Chronological Relationship of the New Testament Books** chart on page 104 shows that the Gospels were not the first New Testament books written. The four Gospels, Matthew, Mark, Luke, and John, cover the history of the birth, life, and death of Jesus Christ from 5 BC to AD 33. They show that God came in a body.

The book of Acts covers the history of the birth of the church. Acts begins in AD 33 and covers the thirty years following Christ's resurrection. It shows that God came by His Spirit to live in our bodies to form His body, the church.

CHRONOLOGICAL RELATIONSHIP OF THE NEW TESTAMENT BOOKS

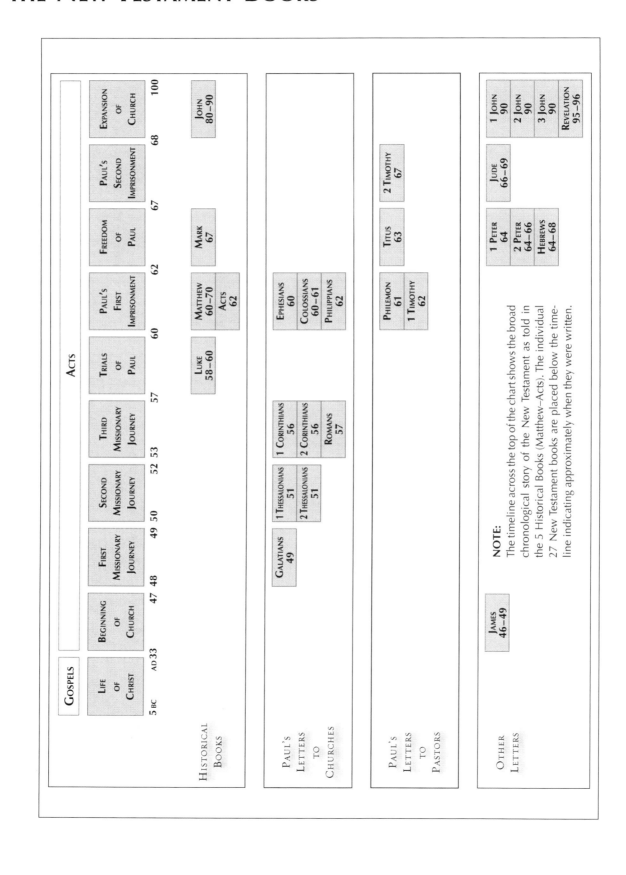

GOSPELS

ACTS

LIFE OF CHRIST	BEGINNING OF CHURCH	FIRST MISSIONARY JOURNEY	SECOND MISSIONARY JOURNEY	THIRD MISSIONARY JOURNEY	TRIALS OF PAUL	PAUL'S FIRST IMPRISONMENT	FREEDOM OF PAUL	PAUL'S SECOND IMPRISONMENT	EXPANSION OF CHURCH
5 BC AD 33	47 48	49 50	52 53	57	60	62	67	68	100

HISTORICAL BOOKS

LUKE 58–60

MATTHEW 60–70
ACTS 62

MARK 67

JOHN 80–90

PAUL'S LETTERS TO CHURCHES

GALATIANS 49

1 THESSALONIANS 51
2 THESSALONIANS 51

1 CORINTHIANS 56
2 CORINTHIANS 56
ROMANS 57

EPHESIANS 60
COLOSSIANS 60–61
PHILIPPIANS 62

PAUL'S LETTERS TO PASTORS

PHILEMON 61
1 TIMOTHY 62

TITUS 63

2 TIMOTHY 67

OTHER LETTERS

JAMES 46–49

1 PETER 64
2 PETER 64–66
HEBREWS 64–68

JUDE 66–69

1 JOHN 90
2 JOHN 90
3 JOHN 90
REVELATION 95–96

NOTE:
The timeline across the top of the chart shows the broad chronological story of the New Testament as told in the 5 Historical Books (Matthew–Acts). The individual 27 New Testament books are placed below the timeline indicating approximately when they were written.

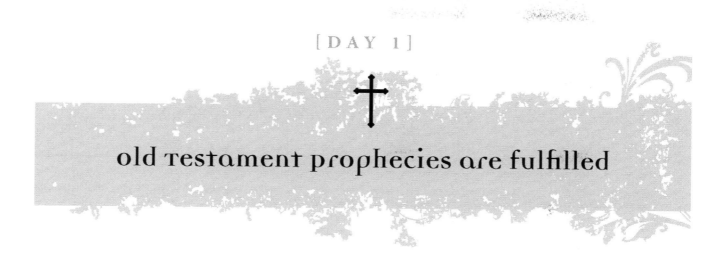

old testament prophecies are fulfilled

Between the Old Testament Prophets and the New Testament Gospels there were four hundred years of silence! There were no more prophets because God did not speak. However, right on time, the silence was broken by the cry of a baby—not just any baby, but the one who fulfilled the three hundred Old Testament prophecies about His coming. God had promised Abraham a descendant who would bless the whole world. The New Testament History books show the coming of that seed by providing the historical record of Jesus, who fulfilled many of the Old Testament prophets' predictions written hundreds of years before.

A. Old Testament prophecies regarding Messiah's birth were fulfilled.

1. The prophet Isaiah (written 740 BC) said Messiah would be born of a virgin (Isaiah 7:14). What was true of Jesus (see Matthew 1:18,21)?

2. Isaiah said a Son would be given, the government would rest on His shoulders, there would be no end to His government, and He would sit on the throne of David (Isaiah 9:6-7). What was true of Jesus (see Matthew 28:18; Luke 1:31-33)?

3. The prophet Micah (735 BC) said Messiah would be born in Bethlehem (Micah 5:2). What was true of Jesus (see Luke 2:4-7)?

B. Old Testament prophecies regarding Messiah's death were fulfilled.

1. The prophet Zechariah (520 BC) said Messiah would come as a king endowed with salvation, humble, and mounted on the foal of a donkey (Zechariah 9:9). What was true of Jesus (see Matthew 21:6-8)?

2. Isaiah said Messiah would be struck, spit on, and humiliated (Isaiah 50:6-7). What was true of Jesus (see Matthew 26:67-68; 27:28-29)?

3. He would be like a sheep silent before shearers (Isaiah 53:7). What was true of Jesus (see Matthew 26:62-63)?

4. He would die with the wicked and be buried with the rich (Isaiah 53:9). What was true of Jesus (see Matthew 27:38,57-60)?

5. He would be valued at thirty shekels of silver, which would be thrown to the potter in the house of the Lord (Zechariah 11:12-13). What was true of Jesus (see Matthew 27:3,7)?

LOVE & WAR QUESTION: What does Jesus' fulfilling so many specific Old Testament prophecies say to you about God?

When God says something, you can count on it!

C. The whole Law and the Prophets depend on love.

In the Old Testament History books, God gave Ten Commandments. The first four dealt with man's relationship with God, and the last six with man's relationship with men.

1. In the New Testament History books, Jesus was asked which is the greatest commandment in the Law. What was His answer (see Matthew 22:36-40)?

2. List three things God says about the future (see Matthew 24:11-13).

If you love Me, you will keep My commandments. (John 14:15)

All through the Scriptures we have seen the love God has for us. We demonstrate our love for God when we obey His commandments. Men constantly make choices to obey or not obey. Adam and Eve were faced with such a choice. Would they eat from the tree in the garden? After they chose to disobey, God provided a way out, but men still had to make a choice. Would they get on the ark? Would they apply the blood of the Passover lamb to their doorposts? Would they get rid of their other gods?

As we obey God, He reveals more of Himself to us (John 14:21). However, false prophets mislead us and cause us to disobey God so our love will grow cold. The Gospels present "good news" to enable us to endure to the end.

REVIEW IT!
Jesus fulfilled the Old Testament prophecies about the Messiah!

matthew and mark

All four gospels provide the history of the life, death, and resurrection of Jesus, our Savior. Have you ever wondered why there are four gospels? In God's great wisdom, He used four different men writing to four different audiences to tell about Jesus from four different perspectives.

Matthew, one of the twelve apostles, included 128 references to the Old Testament, showing how Jesus fulfilled those prophecies about a coming King.

A. Matthew was written to the *Jews* to show Jesus as *King*.
In the Old Testament History, God promised David he would be ruler of Israel and his house and throne would endure forever (2 Samuel 7:8,16).

1. Matthew's genealogy says Jesus is a descendant of which Jewish king (see Matthew 1:1)?

2. What did the Magi say about Jesus? What gifts did they bring (see Matthew 2:1-2,11)?

David was promised an eternal throne. Jesus' genealogy proves Jesus is a legitimate king from the lineage of David. The Magi came looking for the "King of the Jews" and brought Jesus gifts fit for a king.

3. How do we enter Jesus' kingdom (see Matthew 7:13-14)?

Men want to think there are many ways into God's kingdom, but we are told there is one narrow gate. Jesus said, "I am the way, and the truth, and the life; no one comes to the Father but through Me" (John 14:6).

4. What did Matthew warn about prophets (see Matthew 7:15-16)?

5. Who will and who will not enter God's kingdom (see Matthew 7:21-23)?

6. What are we to do regarding His kingdom? Why (see Matthew 6:33)?

Matthew clearly shows Jesus as King. However, Jesus said His kingdom was a different kind of kingdom. Those living in it are not to worry but are to pray for His kingdom to come and His will to be done. Jesus came as "King of the Jews" (Matthew 2:2). However, Israel rejected her King! Is Jesus your King?

LOVE & WAR QUESTION: What did you learn about Jesus and yourself from Matthew?

B. Mark was written to the *Romans* and shows Jesus as *servant*.

There is no genealogy in the gospel of Mark because there is no concern about the historical lineage of a servant. It is a book of action. A repeated word is "immediately." Both Jesus and His followers were continually *doing* because servants act.

1. How did Jesus invite His followers to serve Him (see Mark 1:17)?

2. When and how did His hearers respond (see Mark 1:18)?

3. When Jesus served Simon's mother-in-law by healing her, what did she do (see Mark 1:30-31)?

4. When Jesus' apostles told Him all the acts they had performed, what did He suggest they do? What do servants need (see Mark 6:30-31)?

5. Jesus taught that just as a servant sows seed, the Word of God must be sown in our hearts. What will keep the sown Word from being fruitful?
   a. Mark 4:14-15

   b. Mark 4:16-17

   c. Mark 4:18-19

6. What do you learn about serving (see Mark 10:43-45)?

How or who is God asking you to serve?

Do you consider yourself a servant? To be great we must become servants. We are to serve as Jesus served. He gave Himself for others. Servants lovingly serve because they have the needs of others in mind.

REVIEW IT!
In Matthew Jesus is shown as King. In Mark Jesus is shown as servant.

Luke

Luke was a Gentile physician and, therefore, well qualified to discuss the humanity of Jesus. He began Jesus' genealogy with Adam, the first man.

A. Luke was written to the *Greeks* and shows Jesus as the *perfect man*.

   1. Luke shows Jesus as the perfect man. Describe Jesus' human relationship with His parents (see Luke 2:43-45,48-51).

   2. What do you learn about Jesus' growth as a person (see Luke 2:52)?

   3. What do you learn about your Enemy Satan from his temptation of Jesus (see Luke 4:1-13)?

From Jesus' temptation we see that Satan desires to be worshiped. He attacks where we are weak. All kingdoms of the earth have been handed over to him, so he does control this world temporarily; however, all his attacks can be deflected by the Word of God.

   4. Why did Jesus come as the "Son of Man" (see Luke 19:10)?

5. As Jesus prayed in the Garden of Gethsemane before His crucifixion, what did He experience as a man (see Luke 22:44)?

In His humanity Jesus revealed the love of God in a way we can see and understand. He requires us to love others in the same unconditional manner: "But I say to you who hear, love your enemies, do good to those who hate you, bless those who curse you, pray for those who mistreat you. Whoever hits you on the cheek, offer him the other also; and whoever takes away your coat, do not withhold your shirt from him either" (Luke 6:27-29).

6. As a man, Jesus experienced human physical needs. What was one human need of Jesus (see Luke 8:22-23)?

7. In this same account, what did Jesus do that was not human (see Luke 8:23-25)?

Although he was a man who grew in stature, got tired and hungry, made choices, and felt physical and emotional pain, Jesus was also God, demonstrating supernatural power over nature.

B. It is important that Jesus came as a *man*.
1. God declared, "The wages of sin is death" (Romans 6:23). What did Jesus do to pay this wage (see Luke 23:46)?

2. Even after His resurrection, how did Jesus demonstrate His humanity (see Luke 24:38-43)?

God is eternal and cannot die. Jesus had to come as a man because "the wages of sin is death," and only a man could die!

C. It is important that Jesus came as a *perfect* man.

    1. What did those who observed Jesus' life and suffering on the cross say about His character (see Luke 23:33,39-41,47)?

Jesus had to come as a *perfect* man because only a perfect man would have no sin of His own to pay for; therefore, only sinless Jesus could offer forgiveness for your sins (Luke 24:46-47)!

D. It is important that Jesus is *God*.

As a man Jesus could die, and as a perfect man Jesus could die for you, but only as God can He calm the storms of your life!

What did you learn about Jesus' humanity and your own from Luke?

REVIEW IT!

In Luke Jesus is shown as the perfect man who came to seek and to save the lost.

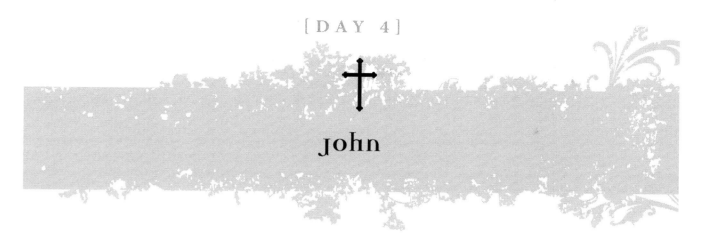

John

Matthew was written to the *Jews* to show Jesus as *King*. Mark was written to the *Romans* to show Jesus as *servant*. Luke was written to the *Greeks* to show Jesus as the *perfect man*.

A. John was written to *everyone* to show Jesus as *God*.

   1. John presents Jesus' genealogy in the first chapter. What is Jesus' family history according to John (see John 1:1,14)?

   2. John claims that Jesus is God in the flesh. What did Jesus claim about Himself? How did the people respond to His claim?
     a. John 5:18

     b. John 10:30-33

When God called Moses to deliver Israel, Moses said the people would ask who sent him. God told Moses His name: "I AM WHO I AM. . . . Thus you shall say to the sons of Israel, 'I AM has sent me to you'" (Exodus 3:13-14).

   3. In the garden, how did Jesus refer to Himself? What happened to the soldiers when they tried to arrest Him (see John 18:4-6)?

By referring to God's eternal name of "I AM," Jesus was claiming to be God. Seven times in John's gospel He referred to Himself this way, with such statements as, "I am the bread of life" (John 6:35,48) and "I am the Light of the world" (John 8:12; 9:5). When the soldiers tried to arrest Jesus after He said, "I am *He*" (John 18:5), they fell back to the ground from the sheer power of His words. They did not take God-in-the-flesh by force; Jesus allowed Himself to be taken to the cross to fulfill the plan of God.

4. Anyone can claim to be God, but Jesus did not just claim; He did miracles to prove His divinity.
    a. What did Jesus do (see John 2:7-10)? How did His disciples respond (see John 2:11)?

    b. What did Jesus do (see John 4:17-18,28-29)? How did the Samaritans respond (see John 4:39)?

    c. What did Jesus do (see John 6:9-11)? How did the people respond (see John 6:14)?

    d. What did Jesus do (see John 9:10-11)? How did the Pharisees respond (see John 9:16)?

    e. What did Jesus do (see John 11:43-44)? How did the Jews respond (see John 11:45)?

John's genealogy says God became flesh and dwelt among us. Jesus not only claimed to be God, but He also did things only God could do. He turned water into wine, healed the sick, multiplied food, forgave sin, and raised the dead! But the response of the people was mixed. Some believed, and some tried to kill Him.

5. What did other people say about Jesus' identity?
    a. What did John the Baptist claim (see John 1:29,32-34)?

b. What did Thomas claim (see John 20:27-28)?

Not only did Jesus claim to be God and do things only God could do, but other people also testified that Jesus is God.

B. John wrote to convince men to believe in Jesus.
According to its author, this last gospel was written "so that you may believe that Jesus is the Christ, the Son of God; and that believing you may have life in His name" (John 20:31).

1. Why did God come in the flesh (see John 3:16)?

2. What is eternal life (see John 17:3)?

LOVE & WAR QUESTION: What does it mean for your life that Jesus is God?

The Gospels tell us the history of the first coming of the Savior, Jesus Christ. They show Jesus is *King, servant, perfect man,* and *God.* Many people think if they could just see Jesus perform a miracle, they would believe; however, the Gospels reveal that although Jesus did a great number of miracles, many who saw them did not believe.

What about you? Do you believe Jesus is fully human and fully divine? Do you believe He alone gives eternal life? Believing with your mind is not enough, for even the demons believe and shudder (see James 2:19-20). The word *believe* means to adhere to, trust in, and rely on. Are you willing to surrender yourself to Jesus and totally rely on Him?

▶ **REVIEW IT!**
In John Jesus came as God to give us eternal life.

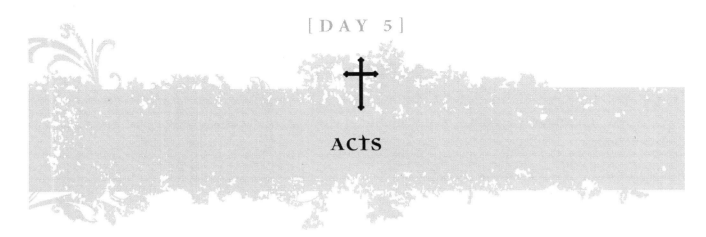

ACTS

The Gospels show the history of God coming in a *physical body* to gain victory over sin and death. Acts shows the coming of God's Spirit to live in *our bodies* to form *His body*. Therefore, Acts is the history of the birth of the church.

Let's review:

▶ *Matthew* reveals Jesus as _____.

▶ *Mark* reveals Jesus as _____.

▶ *Luke* reveals Jesus as _____.

▶ *John* reveals Jesus as _____.

A. Acts is the history of God's *Spirit* coming to form the *church*.
1. What two things did Jesus say would happen when the Holy Spirit came (see Acts 1:8)?

2. What happened at Pentecost when the Holy Spirit came (see Acts 2:4-6)?

B. God's Spirit transforms lives and empowers us to witness.
God said, "You will receive power when the Holy Spirit has come upon you; and you shall be My witnesses both in *Jerusalem*, and in all *Judea* and *Samaria*, and even to the *remotest part of the earth*" (Acts 1:8, emphasis added).

1. God empowered three men whose names begin with *P* to be His witnesses.

   a. Who was God's witness to *Jerusalem and Judea* (see Acts 2:14)?

   b. Who was God's witness to *Samaria* (see Acts 8:5)?

   c. Who was God's witness to the *remotest part of the earth* (see Acts 15:36)?

2. Before the Holy Spirit entered him, how did Saul (Paul) wage war against God (see Acts 8:3)?

3. Paul was once Jesus' enemy. How did he encounter the resurrected Jesus, who gave His life for him (see Acts 9:1-5,8)?

4. How was Paul changed by the power of the Holy Spirit (see Acts 9:17-20)?

5. What did Paul's relationship with Jesus cost him (see Acts 14:19)?

When people don't like the message, they often shoot the messenger! Paul suffered greatly for Jesus Christ but counted everything as loss compared to the value of knowing Christ.

6. Although the Spirit empowered Paul to be a witness, what two seemingly contrary things did the Holy Spirit also do (see Acts 16:6-7)?

7. Where did the Spirit lead him to witness instead (see Acts 16:9-10)?

Paul wanted to go to Asia, but the Spirit steered him to Europe. We, too, receive power from the Holy Spirit to live victoriously and to witness. The Holy Spirit not only changes and empowers us, but He also leads us where He wants us to go and prompts us to do the will of God (Ezekiel 36:27).

8. Can you share a time when God changed the direction of your life?

LOVE & WAR QUESTION: What have you learned about the Holy Spirit from your reading in Acts?

 REVIEW IT!
Acts shows God's Spirit coming to live in us to form the church.

New Testament History

Summary

The New Testament History gospels of *Matthew, Mark, Luke,* and *John* tell the story of Jesus coming in flesh *to live with us* to defeat our enemies of sin and death through His own death and resurrection. They show the Savior fulfilling many Old Testament prophecies:

1. God prophesied a seed of Abraham who would bless the whole world. Jesus is a descendant of Abraham through the tribe of Judah who came to bless the whole world by dying to redeem men.

2. God promised David a kingdom that would be eternal. Jesus is a king from the line of David, and He will reign forever.

3. God foreshadowed Jesus in the Passover lamb that saved all in the household who applied its blood. Jesus Himself is the Lamb of God, who takes away the sin of the world.

The New Testament History book of *Acts* reveals that after His ascension Jesus did not leave us alone but sent the Holy Spirit *to live in us* to fight life's battles. God's Spirit in us not only transforms us as individuals but also unites us to form Christ's body, the church. Therefore, the New Testament History books show God coming in the body of a man so that He might live in our bodies! Acts is the historical link between the Gospels and the New Testament Letters.

> Greater love has no one than this, that one lay down his life for his friends.
> (John 15:13)

▶ The five New Testament History books reveal Jesus as our **Savior**.

New Testament History
Review/Discussion Questions

(You may also use the Love & War Questions from your daily homework for discussion or review.)

1. What did you learn from the personal stories?

2. What did you learn about Jesus in the Gospels?

3. What did you learn about the Holy Spirit?

4. Why is the book of Acts important to us today?

5. What is the most important thing God said to you personally through the New Testament History books, and what are you going to do about it?

#5
New Testament writings

Jesus our teacher

#5 DVD Notes

A Personal Story of
Love and *War*

The Enemy of Suffering

Designers define the classic "kitchen triangle" using the location of the refrigerator, stove, and sink. It is here, they say, that the cook should be able to move quickly and unimpeded. Often my seven-year-old twins, Caroline and Daniel, sit right in the middle of this triangle of space — and I love it. Growing up, I remember our kitchen being the central area where everyone congregated in our home, and I do not want mine to be any different. It is here that many of my most meaningful conversations with my children occur.

One particular Saturday night was no exception. Earlier in the day, my husband and I had taken our twins to see a reenactment of the Revolutionary War's Battle of Cowan's Ford at historic Rural Hill. That evening while washing a pint of strawberries in the kitchen, I explained to Daniel, who was sitting on the floor right next to me, that though the British prevailed in this battle, the Patriot forces ultimately won the war and America's liberty. Fully expecting another question about the American Revolution, my son asked, "Mommy, did God give me my leukemia?" I took a seat beside him and questioned, "What do you think, honey?" He said, "I think Adam and Eve should have listened and obeyed what God said in the first place. Then they could have stayed in that beautiful garden and nobody would ever have to get sick!"

I gave my son the biggest hug and agreed. As a result of man's rebellion we live in a fallen world complete with sin, suffering, and death. But, as I clarified to Daniel, losing a battle is not the same as losing the war!

This life is not all there is, and Jesus defeated death to prove His dominion over all: "When he had disarmed the rulers and authorities, He made a public display of them, having triumphed over them through Him" (Colossians 2:15). Our loving heavenly Father allows tough times to come into our lives for His glory and our good.

As much as God is using my son's illness as an occasion of testing in my life, He is using it in the lives of my children for something far greater. Daniel is experiencing the visible hand of God, and he and his sister, Caroline, are able to see day by day the Lord's interest in every detail of their little lives. What a gift to be convinced so early of God's great love for them.

Before bedtime that evening, I flipped through Lee Strobel's book *The Case for Faith* and found this quote by Peter Kreeft: "God didn't let Job suffer because He lacked love, but because He did love, in order to bring Job to the point of encountering God face to face, which is humanity's supreme happiness. Job's suffering hollowed out a big space in him so that God and joy could fill it."

God's love is not make-believe. It is real. Like Daniel I am discovering that suffering is only a magnifying glass the Lord uses to reveal Himself more closely. Romans 8:35 asks, "Who will separate us from the love of Christ? Will tribulation, or distress, or persecution, or famine, or nakedness, or peril, or sword?" Had it not been for Daniel's cancer and encountering God at this place of extreme need, I would never have understood how absolutely certain the answer is: Nothing and no one can separate me from His love, and in all these things we are more than conquerors through Him who loved us.

New Testament Writings

Overview

But in all these things we overwhelmingly conquer through Him who loved us. For I am convinced that neither death, nor life, nor angels, nor principalities, nor things present, nor things to come, nor powers, nor height, nor depth, nor any other created thing, will be able to separate us from the love of God, which is in Christ Jesus our Lord. (Romans 8:37-39)

▶ These twenty-one New Testament Writing books show Jesus as our **Teacher**:

  ▶ *Paul's Letters to Churches:* Romans, 1 Corinthians, 2 Corinthians, Galatians, Ephesians, Philippians, Colossians, 1 Thessalonians, 2 Thessalonians
  ▶ *Paul's Letters to Pastors:* 1 Timothy, 2 Timothy, Titus, Philemon
  ▶ *Other Letters:* Hebrews, James, 1 Peter, 2 Peter, 1 John, 2 John, 3 John, Jude

The entire Scripture reveals the love God has for us. However, we have struggled to walk in His love because of the enemies we face. When trials come we may think the battle has been lost, but "losing a battle is not the same as losing the war"! As we see in the personal story "The Enemy of Suffering," it is often during life's difficulties that our great God and His love are even more evident.

The battle of belief begins in the mind. "The god of this world has blinded the minds of the unbelieving so that they might not see the light of the gospel of the glory of Christ, who is the image of God" (2 Corinthians 4:4). Satan tries to blind the minds not only of unbelievers but of believers as well because he knows that our beliefs determine our attitudes and our behavior. We behave as we behave because we believe what we believe!

Because a fierce battle rages for our minds, Jesus, our Teacher, wants us to know that "the weapons of our warfare are not of the flesh, but divinely powerful for the destruction of fortresses. . . . We are taking every thought captive to the obedience of Christ" (2 Corinthians 10:4-5).

Let's review:

  ▶ The _____ Old Testament _____ books reveal God as our _____.

  ▶ The _____ Old Testament _____ books reveal God as our _____.

▶ The _____ Old Testament _____ books reveal God as our _____.

▶ The _____ New Testament _____ books reveal Jesus as our _____.

▶ The _twenty-one_ New Testament _Writing_ books reveal Jesus as our **Teacher**.

The five Old Testament Writing books are different forms of poetry giving wisdom for successful living. They tell us *what to believe about God*:

▶ He is sovereign even in suffering (Job).
▶ He is to be worshiped (Psalms).
▶ He gives wisdom for daily life (Proverbs).
▶ Without Him life has no meaning (Ecclesiastes).
▶ He celebrates intimacy in marriage (Song of Solomon).

The New Testament Writing books are not *poetry* but are *letters* written to teach the church or believers by warning and instructing them what to believe and how to behave. The New Testament Letters taught and encouraged the early church, and they teach and encourage us today because we deal with the same enemies: Satan, self, and the world system. We, too, need to know how to discern truth and endure to the end.

The **Chronological Relationship of the New Testament Books** chart on page 104 shows that Paul wrote thirteen of the twenty-one letters. As he traveled he wrote letters to churches in Rome, Corinth, Galatia, Ephesus, Philippi, Colossae, and Thessalonica and to Timothy, Titus, and Philemon as individuals. Paul's letters were named by those receiving them. Paul wrote over a period of fourteen years to believers in various stages of spiritual maturity, and at least five books were penned while Paul was in prison.

The last eight letters are called general epistles or "other letters" because they were written by someone other than Paul. Regardless of the author, God wanted His followers to believe rightly so they would live rightly.

god's purpose for the Letters

At the coming of the Spirit at Pentecost "there were Jews living in Jerusalem, devout men from every nation under heaven" (Acts 2:5). One hundred twenty people were gathered in the upper room when the Holy Spirit came, and they all went home sharing the good news. Peter and others preached in the power of the Holy Spirit, and about five thousand men received the Word at one time, so the church was growing and spreading (Acts 1:15; 4:4; 5:14). Even persecution could not stop it; however, it was imperative that the church grow in truth as well as in number.

God sent men such as Peter, Paul, and John to guard and grow young believers by teaching them truth. The new converts met in local groups to worship and study. The twenty-one New Testament Letters were written to these local churches between AD 45 and 95 to encourage spiritual maturity through the following:

▶ *Sound doctrine* — what we are to believe
▶ *Spiritual disciplines* — what we are to do to grow
▶ *Supernatural devotion* — how we are to love and live

A. Sound doctrine says God has a new dwelling place.
In the Old Testament History books we saw God dwelling in the *garden*, in the *tabernacle*, and finally in the *temple*. In the New Testament History books God dwelt in the *flesh, in Jesus* (John 1:14).

1. Where do the New Testament Letters tell us God now dwells (see 1 Corinthians 3:16)?

2. How does the Holy Spirit enable us to win the battle over sin within (see Galatians 5:16-24)?

The Holy Spirit came upon and indwelt believers at Pentecost. When we receive Jesus, God dwells in us. We become the temple of God!

B. Sound Doctrine Versus Satan's Lies

To keep us from becoming God's temple Satan deceives us through false doctrine. Satan is "a liar and the father of lies" (John 8:44). The most common lie is that we do not need Jesus but can be righteous through a life of good works. However, Paul taught, "There is none righteous, not even one; . . . there is none who does good, there is not even one. . . . For all have sinned and fall short of the glory of God" (Romans 3:10-12,23; reference to Psalm 14:1-3; 53:1-3).

1. Since we are not righteous or good, are we made right with God (saved or made safe) by faith or by works (see Ephesians 2:8-9)?

2. Though we are saved by faith, not works, what does Paul say is true regarding works (see Ephesians 2:10)?

Sound doctrine says we are not saved *by* works but *for* works. James tells us that faith without works is dead and useless (James 2:17,20).

3. Since we are made right by faith, what is the role of the Law (see Romans 3:20)?

The Law gives us knowledge of sin and becomes our tutor to lead us to Christ (Galatians 3:24). The Letters tell us we all need to be "justified" or made "just-if-I'd" never sinned. Being justified, or cleansed of sin by faith in Jesus Christ, always leads to a changed life.

God not only demonstrated His love by dying to deal with our sin but also gave us His Spirit to empower us to fulfill the Law by loving others. Living out the love and life of God is contrary to human nature, but by the power of the Holy Spirit we are able to do so.

C. The early church had problems living out Christ's love.
1. What were some of the problems in the church at Corinth?
   a. 1 Corinthians 1:10-11

b. 1 Corinthians 3:1-3

c. 1 Corinthians 5:1-2

Quarrels, jealousy, spiritual immaturity, and sexual immorality in the church revealed that the early believers were not living Spirit-controlled lives.

2. What were the people in Corinth exhorted to do (see 1 Corinthians 5:6-7)?

God told the people to clean out the sin among them as if it were leaven because a little sin would affect the whole body. God reminded them of Christ, the Passover lamb, who died for every sin.

D. Sound doctrine leads to discernment.
   1. The gospel was defined for the church. There are three parts:
      a. First, what did Jesus do on our behalf (see 1 Corinthians 15:1-3)? According to what Scriptures?

      b. Then what two things happened to Jesus (see 1 Corinthians 15:4)?

      c. Finally what did Jesus do (see 1 Corinthians 15:5-8)?

The gospel, or good news, is this: Jesus died for our sins, was buried, rose on the third day, and appeared to many, just as the Old Testament Scriptures prophesied. Satan, our Enemy, wants to keep us in the dark about the truth of the gospel and what it means for us personally. The truth is, "If you confess with your mouth Jesus as Lord, and believe in your heart that God raised Him from the dead, you will be saved" (Romans 10:9).

Though Satan is darkness, "Satan disguises himself as an angel of light. Therefore it is not surprising if his servants also disguise themselves as servants of righteousness" (2 Corinthians 11:14-15).

2. What was the problem in the church in Galatia (see Galatians 1:6-7)?

The church was challenged by sin within and by false teachers within and without who offered a different gospel other than the one proclaiming that Jesus died, rose again, and was seen by many, as the Old Testament predicted. The New Testament Writings corrected such wrong beliefs and behavior by teaching the truth.

 **LOVE & WAR QUESTION:** How has the truth of the gospel changed your life?

▶ **REVIEW IT!**
The New Testament Letters teach followers of Christ what to believe and how to live.

sound doctrine

Paul was zealously self-righteous and persecuted Christians. Yet on the road to Damascus, he had a personal encounter with the living Jesus. God blinded Paul physically so he could see spiritually! Changed by the Holy Spirit, Paul became as zealous for Christ as he had been against Him. Because Paul loved God, he also loved men! He wrote the first thirteen New Testament Letters to teach believers and to keep them living in truth.

A. Sound doctrine says we are to live in Christ.
Jesus said, "In that day you will know that I am *in* My Father, and you *in* Me, and I *in* you" (John 14:20, emphasis added). The general theme of Paul's letters is that to live victoriously we must *live in Christ.*

1. Romans says we become *righteous in Christ* (Romans 3:22). What happens when we are *in Christ* (see 2 Corinthians 5:17)?

2. What must happen so that Christ can live His life fully *in us* (see Galatians 2:20)?

Just as God was to be the center of the Israelites' lives when He dwelt in the tabernacle, or temple, He is to be the center of our lives today. Freedom comes when we die to self and *live in Christ.* Galatians teaches that we are *free in Christ* (Galatians 5:1). However, the Galatians were not experiencing their freedom. Listening to false teaching, they returned to the bondage of the Law. They embraced a different gospel that said salvation was attained by adding their own good works to the completed work of Jesus Christ. The Letters make clear that salvation is by Jesus' sacrifice *plus nothing* and that changed lives are proof of salvation!

3. Though we are free from the Law, *in Christ* what will we do (see Galatians 5:13-14)?

4. How can we love our neighbor and live in freedom (see Galatians 5:18,22-23)?

Romans says we are *righteous* in Christ. Corinthians says we are *made new* in Him. Galatians declares us *free*, and Colossians says we are *complete, or perfect,* in Christ (Colossians 1:27-28). Therefore, the New Testament Letters teach that *in Christ* we are made righteous, new, free, and complete. Nothing more is needed for our salvation!

B. God has given us armor for the battle.
   1. When we are *in Christ* God gives us armor. Why is the armor of God important? What do you learn about your battle (see Ephesians 6:11-13)?

   2. What piece of armor protects our heart from Satan's arrows (see Ephesians 6:16)?

   3. What armor protects our minds (see Ephesians 6:17)?

LOVE & WAR QUESTION: What does it mean to you to be *in Christ*?

C. The other authors affirm true doctrines about Jesus.

    1. List truths the Letters taught the young church about Jesus.

        a. Hebrews 1:1-3 (What did the Father call the Son in Hebrews 1:8?)

        b. Hebrews 7:24-26

        c. Hebrews 13:5

        d. Hebrews 13:8

Jesus not only is God, who purified us from our sin, but He is also our eternal High Priest, always interceding with the Father for us. The Old Testament priests never sat down because their job was never done, but Jesus sat down at God's right hand because His sacrifice paid for sin once and for all. Jesus is unchanging and promises to never leave us.

    2. List truths the Letters teach about Jesus and the Devil.

        a. Hebrews 2:14

        b. 1 John 3:8

Sound doctrine says that God's Spirit lives in believers, while Satan and his spirits live in the world. The Letters remind us that Jesus is the Creator, who took on flesh and died to destroy the work of the Devil! Although the Devil and his spirits are at work in the world, God assures us we "have overcome them; because greater is He who is *in you* than he who is in the world" (1 John 4:4, emphasis added).

REVIEW IT!
Sound doctrine assures us that we are new, complete, and have overcome *in Christ*.

spiritual disciplines

Christianity was a new concept that said we are made right by faith, not works; to gain, we must give; and to live, we must die! There were false teachers trying to infiltrate the churches, so Christians needed to know the truth. There was much persecution, so they needed the discipline to grow so they would endure to the end.

A. The spiritual disciplines take discipline.
    1. Record how Paul told young Timothy to live or behave.
        a. 1 Timothy 4:7-8

        b. 1 Timothy 4:12

    2. Paul spoke of endurance. List what we are to do (the "if" clauses) and what will happen if we do so (see 2 Timothy 2:11-13).

    3. What discipline does God require regarding His Word?
        a. 2 Timothy 2:15

        b. 2 Timothy 3:16-17

4. What three things does God's Spirit give us (see 2 Timothy 1:7)?

"But we all, with unveiled face, beholding as in a mirror the glory of the Lord, are being transformed into the same image from glory to glory, just as from the Lord, the Spirit" (2 Corinthians 3:18). The Letters assure us that when God's Spirit lives in us He transforms us into God's image! However, we must "fight the good fight of faith" (1 Timothy 6:12).

B. The spiritual disciplines win the battle for our minds.

1. We are not to walk in the futility of a mind ignorant of God because of a hard heart (Ephesians 4:17-18). What does submission to God do for your mind (see Romans 12:1-2)?

The problem with a living sacrifice is that it keeps crawling off the altar! Instead of having a renewed mind due to knowing the will of God, our mind is made up — we want our own way!

2. What does choosing to rejoice and pray with thanksgiving in every situation do for your mind (see Philippians 4:4,6-7)?

Our life *in Christ* will be different from those who are not *in Christ* because we will have a new mind-set. As we present our bodies as living sacrifices, God will *renew our minds* so our thoughts are His. As we pray and praise God, His peace will *guard our minds* so we are not anxious. Philippians teaches it is even possible to have *joy in Christ* regardless of our circumstances. Therefore, *in Christ* we can face life's difficulties with a brand-new way of thinking!

C. Spiritual disciplines are needed during trials.

1. What disciplines do you need to run life's race or fight your battles?
   a. Hebrews 12:1

   b. Hebrews 12:2-3

We must lay aside those things that trip us up and keep our eyes on Jesus so we can run with endurance and not grow weary or get discouraged.

    2. List what we are to do in the battle of suffering and the reason, if the passage gives it. (Note the references to our Enemy, the Devil.)
       a. James 1:2-3

       b. James 4:7

       c. James 5:13

       d. 1 Peter 5:6-7

       e. 1 Peter 5:8-10

Since there is an adversary prowling around seeking to devour us, we can see why the spiritual disciplines of submission, prayer, and praise are so vitally important. It is necessary to humble ourselves under the mighty hand of God and resist the Devil so he will flee (James 4:7).

D. The Letters teach spiritual disciplines to enable us to endure.
    1. What are the three disciplines necessary to keep winning our battles?
       a. 1 Peter 2:2

       b. 1 Thessalonians 5:17-18

c. Hebrews 10:24-25

It takes discipline to pray without ceasing, to regularly meet with other believers, and to fill our minds with God's Word. However, we need the communication with God and accountability with others to remain strong and protected from deception. In addition to prayer, Bible study, and regularly meeting with others, another discipline is to be quiet and listen to God. "Be still, and know that I am God" (Psalm 46:10, KJV).

 LOVE & WAR QUESTION: What are some spiritual disciplines necessary for you to grow in truth? How are you doing with these?

 REVIEW IT!
Spiritual disciplines determine spiritual success.

supernatural Devotion

Some form of the word *love* is used 156 times in the twenty-one New Testament Letters! Jesus sent us love letters so we might become love letters to others.

A. *In Christ* we can have supernatural love, or devotion.
1. When we are right with God, how can we love others (see Romans 5:1,5)?

2. How do we know God loves us (see Romans 5:8)?

3. What does Romans 13:8,10 add to your understanding of love and the Law?

B. *In Christ* we have His power to love as He loves.
1. Explain how we are to live when God's Spirit lives in us.
   a. Ephesians 4:1-3

   b. Ephesians 5:2-4

God has sealed us with His Spirit so we can live a changed life. "Walk by the Spirit, and you will not carry out the desire of the flesh" (Galatians 5:16).

C. We need to live out God's love in our relationships.

1. How are we to live in our marriages (see Ephesians 5:33)?

Men need respect, and women need love! That is the way God made us.

2. How are we to live as children or parents (see Ephesians 6:1-4)?

Relationships are difficult! Children need discipline given out of a heart of love. We teach our children and others by instructing them in God's Word, but equally important is living the Word before them.

D. Characteristics of Christian Love

1. List the characteristics of love that are to be demonstrated in your life (see Colossians 3:12-13).

2. What must we do to have Christian love (see Colossians 3:14-16)?

3. How are we to live with others? What fulfills the Law (see Galatians 6:1-2)?

Sometimes it is hardest to love in our homes and in the church. We can be very gracious to outsiders, but with family it's a different story. Even the early church experienced divisions and competition. Too many churches today are divided over what kind of music to sing or what color the walls should be painted! The Letters teach us what to believe and how we are to behave.

E. If we love God, we'll love others.

    1. How can you discern a true believer?

        a. 1 John 2:15

        b. 1 John 4:7-8

        c. 1 John 4:12,19

Obedience to God is a test of our love for Him. He says, "If you love Me, you will keep My commandments" (John 14:15). *However, another test of our love for God is our love for others.* "And this commandment we have from Him, that the one who loves God should love his brother also" (1 John 4:21).

We cannot love on our own; if we do, our love will be conditional at best. However, because God *is* love, as we live in Christ and He lives in us, His unconditional love will flow through us, proving we belong to Him.

 LOVE & WAR QUESTION: If you are to live out Christ's life and love in your church, home, neighborhood, or workplace, what has to change?

▶ **REVIEW IT!**
Supernatural devotion is a result of Christ living in you.

truth for the present and the future

The New Testament Letters teach sound doctrine, spiritual disciplines, and supernatural devotion, enabling us to live godly lives now and endure in the future.

A. We need supernatural devotion in our daily living.

1. How are older men to live (see Titus 2:2)?

2. How are older women to live (see Titus 2:3-4)?

3. How are younger women to live (see Titus 2:4-5)?

4. Why are older women instructed to encourage younger women to live purely and to love their families (see Titus 2:5)?

Interestingly, in this passage the word for love in the Greek is *phileo*, which means brotherly love. Older women are to teach younger women to be as kindhearted with their husbands and children as they are with friends! Do you treat your family as kindly as you do your friends?

5. How are young men to live and why (see Titus 2:6-8)?

Regardless of our age or gender, God desires for us to live in His love so that Satan and those not *in Christ* will have nothing bad to say about us — or about Him. However, we too often love things rather than people, which can lead to great trouble. "For the love of money is a root of all sorts of evil, and some by longing for it have wandered away from the faith and pierced themselves with many griefs" (1 Timothy 6:10).

LOVE & WAR QUESTION: Summarize what you've learned about love in the Letters.

B. We need sound doctrine to endure.
The Letters teach about the last days: "But the Spirit explicitly says that in later times some will fall away from the faith, paying attention to deceitful spirits and doctrines of demons" (1 Timothy 4:1). God also warned that difficult times will come.

1. List what men will love (see 2 Timothy 3:2-4).

2. Those who love self, money, and pleasure may look religious, but what is really true about their spiritual lives (see 2 Timothy 3:5)?

3. What will happen to those desiring to live godly lives (see 2 Timothy 3:12)?

C. We need sound doctrine to counter false teaching and to prepare for the future.
Some of the Letters were written after Paul's imprisonment and during a time of severe persecution. The church was suffering. False teachers were trying to destroy believers' faith. These Christ followers needed encouragement to endure to the end.

1. What did Peter warn about false teachers (see 2 Peter 2:1-3)?

2. What does 2 Peter 3:9-10 say about God's future judgment?

3. Since Jesus will come again to judge, how are we to live (see 2 Peter 3:11,14)?

4. How did false teachers get in the church? According to Jude, what did they do there (see Jude 4)?

5. List additional insights Jude 18-19 reveals regarding false teachers.

6. To counter false teachers how are you to live (see Jude 20-21)?

The battle begins in the mind! Peter warned, "Be on guard so that you are not carried away by the error of unprincipled men" (2 Peter 3:17). The Letters teach us God's truth to guard us against deception. However, truth is not just to be believed; it is also to be lived out. God follows teaching about future events with encouragement to live godly lives in the present. In other words, what we believe will affect how we live. Knowing Jesus is coming again to judge sin should motivate us to live well.

 LOVE & WAR QUESTION: What additional truth have you received about how to win your spiritual battles?

 REVIEW IT!
You behave as you behave because you believe as you believe.

new testament writings (Letters)

Summary

The New Testament Writings are truly love letters from God sent to teach all believers to have *sound doctrine, spiritual disciplines*, and *supernatural devotion*. We are to love and live to reflect *Christ in us, the hope of glory*.

Because of many false teachers, the early church was prey to confusion and deception. Therefore, these new believers needed to put on the armor of truth, righteousness, faith, the Word of God, and prayer (Ephesians 6:14-18). We need that same armor today!

Paul wanted us to know the protection and power we have in Christ:

▶ We are *righteous* in Christ (Romans 3:22).
▶ We are *alive* in Christ (1 Corinthians 15:22).
▶ We are *new creatures* in Christ (2 Corinthians 5:17).
▶ We are *free* in Christ (Galatians 2:4).
▶ We are *chosen to walk* in Christ (Ephesians 1:4; 2:10).
▶ We are *joyful* in Christ (Philippians 4:10-11).
▶ We are *complete/perfect* in Christ (Colossians 2:9-10).
▶ We are *safe* at Christ's coming (1 Thessalonians 4:13-18).
▶ We have *relief/rest* at Christ's coming (2 Thessalonians 1:7).

In addition to the false teachers, great persecution was making it difficult for the early church to persevere. The Letters teach that in spite of any trials we face, God is still on the throne.

> But in all these things we overwhelmingly conquer through Him who loved us. For I am convinced that neither death, nor life, nor angels, nor principalities, nor things present, nor things to come, nor powers, nor height, nor depth, nor any other created thing, will be able to separate us from the love of God, which is in Christ Jesus our Lord. (Romans 8:37-39)

▶ The twenty-one New Testament Writing books show Jesus as our **Teacher**.

New Testament writings (Letters)
Review/Discussion Questions

(You may also use the Love & War Questions from your daily homework for discussion or review.)

1. What did you learn through the personal stories?

2. What problems did the early church face that we face today (or may face in the future)?

3. What did you learn about having a right mind, especially during trials?

4. What did you learn about each of the following?

   Doctrines

   Disciplines

   Devotion (love)

   Deceivers (false teachers)

#6
new testament prophecy

jesus our victorious king

#6 DVD Notes

A Personal Story of
Love and *War*

THE ENEMIES ARE DEFEATED

I have a good memory. I can remember events that happened when I was two years of age and can even recall trying to get out of my crib; however, I have no memory of my father. He passed away when I was two. Even in my child's mind I knew there was something important I did not have.

Mom was only twenty-five when he died, and she did all she could to support us. However, she had little time to spend with me and no patience with a young boy, so I spent years entertaining myself and was alone much of the time. I remember waking up one night feeling lonely and terrified. I cried out to my mother, who told me to pray to Jesus. To this day I cannot explain how I knew who that was or how I understood the authority of that name, but I prayed to Jesus and never felt terrified like that again. Though I did not fully know Him, He was there when I called.

My mom and I moved to California for a better professional opportunity for her. I remember in first grade hearing the kids talk about fishing, vacations, and flying kites with their dads. I was perplexed by this "dad thing." Finally I asked my mother why I did not have a dad. She choked up and simply said, "Your father died." I finally knew what I was missing, but there was nothing I could do about it. Helpless, I felt a void in my life that I thought could never be filled since I had lost the one and only father I could ever have.

In third grade my mother enrolled me in military school, and I thought it was cool to wear a uniform. She thought I could use a strong male figure in my life. However, the loneliness continued. I would live confined on campus during the week and go home on weekends. Many weekends my mom and I stayed at the home of the man who would later become my stepfather. When we did this I would not see my home, room, or toys for weeks. Because I had no interest in hanging around a man who was not my father and did little to make me feel comfortable, I would ride my bike on the beach all day and avoid everyone. My home and family were the military school and its disciplines. Consequently, I had no sense of what a close, loving family was like.

My mother heard about another military school, and for no logical reason I felt compelled to go there. Unknown to us, this school was run by God-fearing Christians. During an evening Bible study on the book of Revelation, I was confronted with the truth about Jesus. I realized that just because I believed there was a God, had a denominational heritage of sorts, and had been exposed to my mother's religious beliefs did not necessarily mean I believed in Jesus. I had yet to understand the hopelessness of the human condition. I had yet to recognize my imperfections and believe that the remedy is the sacrificial death and resurrection of Jesus Christ. I had yet to give my life to Him. That night I put my faith and my eternal destiny in the One who simply stood at my heart's door and knocked.

Looking back, I can see that Christ was knocking all along. He knocked in the words of my mother, even though she did not fully understand the power of the mere expression of the name of Jesus. He knocked in the way His name resonated in my mind and heart even as a child. He was knocking in the decisions for me to go to schools away from home where the Word was spoken, drawing me away from our empty religious traditions and into a dynamic relationship with a loving Creator. When I was alone for years and had no real sense of friends, family, or a father's existence and love, Christ was knocking by revealing my need. He was always there, and now I know I have a loving heavenly Father and I will live with Him in perfect peace forever.

New Testament prophecy

Overview

And I saw heaven opened, and behold, a white horse, and He who sat on it is called Faithful and True, and in righteousness He judges and wages war. . . . He is clothed with a robe dipped in blood, and His name is called The Word of God. And the armies which are in heaven, clothed in fine linen, white and clean, were following Him on white horses. (Revelation 19:11,13-14)

▶ The one book of New Testament Prophecy, Revelation, shows Jesus as our **Victorious King**.

Even little children experience battles in life . . . battles with loneliness and fear. The loss of a father is a particularly difficult battle to overcome, yet God offers Himself not only as a heavenly Father but also as a Victorious King.

War is a word that evokes fear in every heart. We long for peace, and yet peace does not come. In 1918, World War I ended. It was called the War to End All Wars, but it didn't. Only twenty-one years later the world would once again be embroiled in conflict.

In His Word God has made several things clear:

1. We were not made for war, death, and destruction; we were made for peace and love.
2. The day will come when there will be a final war.
3. That war will be followed by permanent peace. The lion will lay down with the lamb, and weapons will be made into plows.

Satan is not our ruler, and this present world, ruled by Satan, is not our home.

The book of Revelation is God's final written word to His people. It is a book of prophecy that foretells what will take place at the end of time. There is no need for additional revelation because this book details the culmination of God's redemptive love story.

Revelation gives us confidence for the future because we know that God will ultimately be victorious. He will bring about a new world with no tears, no death, no cancer, no suffering, no loneliness, no divorce, and no more battles! He has promised it, and it will come to pass.

God has given us the armor of truth and the helmet of salvation to protect our minds, the breastplate of righteousness and the shield of faith to protect our hearts, and one weapon for offense — the sword of the Spirit, which is His Word.

His Word of truth is to be read, studied, and obeyed. However, it is more than a manual for living; it is a love letter from God, who loves His children passionately. Make it your heart's desire to know Him. Read each word of His as if it were written just for you, because it was! Only by taking up the sword of the Spirit, God's Word, will we be able to stand firm and defeat all enemies. The Word of God assures us that the victory can be won!

One final review:

▶ The _____ Old Testament _____ books reveal God as our _____.

▶ The _____ Old Testament _____ books reveal God as our _____.

▶ The _____ Old Testament _____ books reveal God as our _____.

▶ The _____ New Testament _____ books reveal Jesus as our _____.

▶ The _____ New Testament _____ books reveal Jesus as our _____.

▶ The *one* New Testament *Prophecy* book reveals Jesus as our **Victorious King**.

god's final message

It is important to know that Revelation has been interpreted in many ways:

1. Some believe the prophecies it contains were fulfilled during John's time, so it is now history.
2. Others believe it provides a panorama of church history from John's time until the end.
3. Others believe it is an allegory of the conflict between good and evil.
4. Others accept it as literally prophetic of events that will take place in the future.

We will approach this study from the last perspective, that these are prophecies from God that are yet to be fulfilled. They are promises of what will come to give us a future and a hope!

A. God's Purpose for Sending the Revelation

1. Why was the book of Revelation written (see Revelation 1:1)? (A bond-servant is a slave who has been set free yet chooses to remain with his master to serve. All believers are to be bond-servants.)

2. Who was the writer of Revelation, and why was he on the island of Patmos (see Revelation 1:1-2,9)?

3. What promise is given for those who read and obey this book (see Revelation 1:3)?

4. List the three things John was instructed to write (see Revelation 1:19).

John was to write "the things which you have seen, and the things which are, and the things which will take place after these things" (Revelation 1:19).

The **Chronological Relationship of the New Testament Books** chart on page 104 shows that Revelation, which means "unveiling," was the last book of the Bible written, probably in AD 95–96. Its author, John, was Jesus' disciple and friend who had been exiled to the island of Patmos because of the Word of God and his testimony for Jesus. There God revealed, or unveiled, Himself as the resurrected Christ with the power and authority to judge the world. Jesus revealed to John "the things which you have seen" so that he could share them with us.

B. John saw the resurrected Jesus.
   1. What did John predict about Jesus' return (see Revelation 1:7-8)?

   2. In a sentence, describe the resurrected Jesus seen by John (see Revelation 1:12-16).

   3. What did John do when he saw Jesus (see Revelation 1:17)?

Though John had known Jesus intimately, he fell down like a dead man at the appearance of the resurrected Jesus, no longer a lowly carpenter or a suffering servant but the risen Lord in all His glory.

C. John saw a glimpse into heaven.
   1. In a few sentences describe what John saw and heard in heaven (see Revelation 4:2-4,8).

2. What did the twenty-four elders do and say (see Revelation 4:10-11)?

 What feelings about Jesus do these revelations of John stir in your heart?

God will not cede His glory and authority to another. Jesus is worthy to receive all of our glory, honor, and thanks. Some day we, too, will fall before Him, casting any crowns we have received before His throne to worship and praise Him forever! (Are you getting in practice now?)

 REVIEW IT!
Jesus is worthy to receive our worship and praise.

the seven Letters to seven churches

We have seen that throughout history God has warned in advance that there will be blessing for obedience and cursing for disobedience. John heard Jesus dictate seven letters to seven churches that existed at the time of Revelation. These messages contained both warning and encouragement for their recipients and for us today. John said he wrote of the "things which are."

A. The Letter Written to the Church in *Ephesus*

1. List the reasons Jesus praised those in Ephesus (see Revelation 2:2-3).

2. What did He have against them (see Revelation 2:4)?

B. The Letter Written to the Church in *Smyrna*

1. What was Jesus' encouragement to the church in Smyrna (see Revelation 2:9,11)?

2. What did Jesus warn? What did He encourage believers in Smyrna to do and why (see Revelation 2:10)?

C. The Letter Written to the Church in *Pergamum*

    1. For what did Jesus praise those in Pergamum (see Revelation 2:13)?

    2. What did He have against them? What did He say they should do and why (see Revelation 2:14,16)? (As recorded in Numbers 25:1-3; 31:15-17; Deuteronomy 7:3-4, Balaam, a false prophet for hire, encouraged intermarriage, which resulted in idolatry as God had warned!)

D. The Letter Written to the Church in *Thyatira*

    1. For what did Jesus praise those in Thyatira (see Revelation 2:19)?

    2. What did He have against them (see Revelation 2:20)? (As recorded in 1 Kings 21:25-26, Jezebel introduced pagan religion to Israel.)

E. The Letter Written to the Church in *Sardis*

    1. List what Jesus told the church in Sardis to do and why (see Revelation 3:2-3).

    2. Why did Jesus praise a few of those in Sardis? What three things did He promise these overcomers (see Revelation 3:4-5)?

F. The Letter Written to the Church in *Philadelphia*

1. For what did Jesus praise those in Philadelphia (see Revelation 3:8)?

2. What did Jesus promise them (see Revelation 3:10-11)?

G. The Letter Written to the Church in *Laodicea*

1. What did Jesus have against the church in Laodicea (see Revelation 3:15-16)?

2. On the chart list what God does and what man is called to do in response (see Revelation 3:19-22).

What God Does	What Man Is Called to Do

What message does God have for you or your church from His messages to these churches?

Through the prophecy in Revelation Jesus warns us not to let our love for Him grow cold. If we are only lukewarm, He will spit us out of His mouth. Therefore we must be sensitive to sin and repent. He warns of persecution and the need for perseverance, exhorting believers to remain faithful to the end. He warns His followers not to tolerate false teachers who promote worldliness.

How are you doing in light of these warnings?

REVIEW IT!
God warns and encourages us to endure to the end.

god's judgments

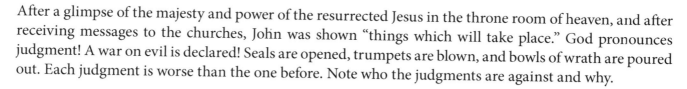

After a glimpse of the majesty and power of the resurrected Jesus in the throne room of heaven, and after receiving messages to the churches, John was shown "things which will take place." God pronounces judgment! A war on evil is declared! Seals are opened, trumpets are blown, and bowls of wrath are poured out. Each judgment is worse than the one before. Note who the judgments are against and why.

A. There are seven seal judgments.

1. Who is worthy to open the book and break the seals? Why (see Revelation 5:5,8-9)?

2. Four of the seals are described as horsemen bringing war, famine, and death. Though great terror follows, what is the response of those who reject Jesus (see Revelation 6:15-17)?

3. Even though seals of judgment are unleashed on the earth, what is revealed about those who come to Jesus through this great tribulation (see Revelation 7:13-17)?

B. There are seven trumpet judgments.

1. The trumpet judgments follow the seal judgments and are more intense. The first trumpet sounded brings hail and fire, and a third of the earth is burned up. This trumpet is followed by six others. John wrote that the sea will become blood and a third of the sea creatures will die; a third of the sun, moon, and stars will be darkened; demons will be released; and a third of mankind will also die (Revelation 8:7–9:19). In spite of these coming horrors, what will unsaved men not do (see Revelation 9:20-21)?

2. God allows us to see a war in heaven between Michael (the archangel of Jude 9) and his angels and Satan and his angels. Record what you learn about your Enemy, the Devil (see Revelation 12:7-10).

3. Jesus has God's authority (Revelation 12:10). How can Satan be overcome (see Revelation 12:11)?

4. In addition to the dragon (Satan), there is another enemy in this end-times battle who has been given authority from Satan. Record what you learn about him (see Revelation 13:2-8).

5. There is a third beast in John's vision. What do you learn about him (see Revelation 13:11-17)?

Satan, our Enemy, is a murderer, a liar, and the father of lies, who counterfeits all truth, including the nature of the triune God. The dragon is Satan (Revelation 12:9). The other parts of the "unholy trinity" are often called the Beast or Antichrist (Revelation 13:1-10) and the False Prophet (Revelation 13:11-18).

Remember, the Old Testament History books told us that signs and miracles alone do not prove a prophet is authentic or true. Satan has great authority and power and even does miracles, but God, our Victorious King, is not finished with him yet!

6. Men still make choices. What will happen to those who choose to follow the counterfeit Christ in the last days (see Revelation 14:9-10)?

LOVE & WAR QUESTION: What new thoughts do you have about your Enemy, Satan?

C. There are seven bowl judgments.

1. The trumpet judgments are followed by the bowl judgments. What are the bowl judgments, and who do they affect (see Revelation 16:1-2)?

All these judgments will be on those who have rejected Jesus! The bowls are judgments for those who worship the Beast. There will be malignant sores, the seas will become blood and every sea creature will die, and the sun will scorch men with fierce heat. God will judge all His enemies and provide for all His saints.

2. What will men do and not do in response to these judgments (see Revelation 16:9)?

Divine wrath is not a popular subject today. Most people don't even want to consider it. However, a study of the Bible's concordance will show there are more references in Scripture to the anger and wrath of God than there are to His love and compassion.

Over the past six weeks we have seen many references to God's love; in fact, God is love. However, God also has righteous anger. He cannot overlook sin but instead has promised to judge it. In pride,

Satan desired to be like God. In our pride, we also desire to live apart from God and rule ourselves! We can either accept the fact that Jesus was judged in our place or choose to deny Him and experience the wrath of God. All men are faced with this choice. No other alternatives exist.

From Revelation and the Old Testament prophets, we see that the day of the Lord is coming when God's final judgment will take place. God will bring an end to wickedness (Isaiah 13:6-13) and spread the gospel to the whole world (Matthew 24:14).

LOVE & WAR QUESTION: Summarize what you've learned about God and the coming judgments.

REVIEW IT!
God's day of wrath is coming, but Jesus is our way of escape.

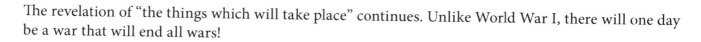

the final war

The revelation of "the things which will take place" continues. Unlike World War I, there will one day be a war that will end all wars!

A. The final war against the world's evil begins.

1. Record what will happen before the war (see Revelation 16:13-14).

2. Describe what will happen next (see Revelation 17:14).

3. Babylon is both an actual city and a picture of the world system Satan fosters that draws men to a life of immorality and sensuousness where luxury, wealth, culture, knowledge, and craftsmanship are valued and worshiped over God (Revelation 18). Babylon is described as "a dwelling place of demons" (Revelation 18:2). What will happen to her (see Revelation 18:9-10)?

4. How will heaven respond to the defeat of Babylon (see Revelation 19:1-2)?

5. What will heaven declare (see Revelation 19:6)?

B. Invitations are issued for a heavenly wedding.

> Husbands, love your wives, just as Christ also loved the church and gave Himself up for her, so that He might sanctify her, having cleansed her by the washing of water with the word, that He might present to Himself the church in all her glory, having no spot or wrinkle or any such thing; but that she would be holy and blameless. (Ephesians 5:25-27)

1. Describe the wedding that follows the battle. How will the bride be dressed (see Revelation 19:7-9)?

2. Describe Jesus' return. How will He come? What will He do? How will He look (see Revelation 19:11,15-16)?

3. Who will come with Jesus, the "Word of God," to fight alongside Him? How will these companions be dressed (see Revelation 19:13-14)?

C. The battle against evil is finally finished.
1. What will happen to the Beast (Antichrist) and the False Prophet (see Revelation 19:19-20)?

2. What will happen to Satan (see Revelation 20:2-3)?

3. What will happen to the martyrs of the end times who don't worship the Beast (see Revelation 20:4)?

4. After the thousand years, what will be the final victory of God over Satan (see Revelation 20:7-10)?

Through a series of judgments and war, God will one day destroy all His enemies. Finally peace on earth will be possible, as all those waging war with God and the saints (or those *in Christ*) will be defeated.

LOVE & WAR QUESTION: How does the final war give comfort and assurance for the future?

▶ **REVIEW IT!**
The Devil has great wrath knowing that his time is short (Revelation 12:12).

the final victory!

While Moses was on the mountain receiving the Ten Commandments (including warnings to have no other gods), Israel was down below making a golden calf! Knowing their God was a jealous God, Moses threw the calf idol into the fire, but God sent judgment for their blatant disobedience, and three thousand men died that day. Moses said to the Lord, "'This people has committed a great sin, and they have made a god of gold for themselves. But now, if You will, forgive their sin — and if not, please *blot me out from Your book which You have written!*' The LORD said to Moses, 'Whoever has sinned against Me, I will blot him out of My book'" (Exodus 32:31-33, emphasis added).

A. God keeps perfect records.

1. At the white throne judgment God will judge those who reject Christ. The throne is white because with no blood covering their sin, people will be judged by God's pure holiness. What do you learn about God's books that are opened at the white throne (see Revelation 20:11-12,15)?

God has at least two books, the Book of Life and a book of deeds. Is the Lamb's Book of Life the same one God and Moses discussed? Since every name would be blotted out because "all have sinned" (Romans 3:23), could it be that when we accept Jesus, who dealt with sin, our names are written — or perhaps rewritten — in the Lamb's Book of Life?

Everyone's deeds will be judged! Romans 14 says, "We will all stand before the judgment seat of God. . . . So then each one of us will give an account of himself to God" (Romans 14:10,12). Believers who have trusted Christ for their salvation will be judged for their deeds, and those works surviving the test of fire will be rewarded (1 Corinthians 3:11-15). However, believers' sin will not be judged because Jesus has already dealt with it on the cross.

Unbelievers, or those who reject Christ, will also be judged for their deeds. However, anyone whose name is *not* found written in the Book of Life will then be thrown into the lake of fire (Revelation 20:15)!

B. There will be a new heaven and a new earth.

1. Describe what will *not* be found in the new heaven and new earth (see Revelation 21:1,4).

2. What *will* be there (see Revelation 21:2-3)?

God first lived with men *in the garden* and then dwelled in their midst *in the tabernacle* and *in the temple*. Then He came near *in the person of His Son, Jesus*, and now He abides *in us by His Holy Spirit*. In the new heaven and new earth God will once more dwell among His people! He will remove death, crying, and pain. The old world and its evils will be gone forever. The One sitting on the throne says, "I am making all things new" (Revelation 21:5)!

3. Who will reside in the new heaven and new earth, and who will not be there (see Revelation 21:27)?

Only those whose names are in the Lamb's Book of Life will experience the new heaven and new earth! We see the eternal importance of God's act of love in sending His Son, Jesus, to die for us and in sending His Spirit to dwell in us. We also see the eternal importance of our decision to accept or reject Christ. Remember, He promised never to leave us or forsake us!

4. The new holy city will have a wall, gates, and streets made of precious stones and pure gold. List what will not be there and why (see Revelation 21:22-23).

5. The New Jerusalem will also have the throne of God and the Lamb, the river of the water of life, and the Tree of Life. What will be missing (see Revelation 22:2-4)?

The throne of God will be there, as will the Tree of Life that was blocked from men in the garden; however, the curse will be removed (Genesis 3:22-24). There will be no more separation and no more death. Therefore, God's bond-servants' great joy will be to see God's face at last! God told Moses, "You cannot see My face, for no man can see Me and live!" (Exodus 33:20). Apparently only redeemed, restored men can look upon the pure holiness of God.

6. What does Jesus promise (see Revelation 22:12)?

7. Sin caused the first family to be separated from the Tree of Life in the Garden of Eden. How are those who now have access to the Tree of Life dressed (see Revelation 22:14)?

Sin also caused men to lose their covering of righteousness, resulting in nakedness and shame. Jesus covers us with a robe of righteousness and promises that those wearing clean robes will once more have access to the Tree of Life.

8. What does Jesus warn regarding the prophecies of Revelation (see Revelation 22:18-19)?

I will rejoice greatly in the LORD,
    My soul will exult in my God;
    For He has clothed me with *garments of salvation*,
    He has wrapped me with a *robe of righteousness*,
    As a bridegroom decks himself with a garland,
    And *as a bride adorns herself* with her jewels. (Isaiah 61:10, emphasis added)

Our Victorious King is coming to destroy His enemies and to be united with His bride; however, we must be rightly dressed for the wedding! Have you allowed Jesus to clothe you with His garments of salvation and with His robe of righteousness? Are you washed and clean? Get ready because Jesus says, "Yes, I am coming quickly" (Revelation 22:20).

Come, Lord Jesus!

What is the most important thing you have learned from this study of love and war?

REVIEW IT!
Jesus is coming soon. In the war to end all wars, the Lamb's team wins!

New Testament Prophecy

Summary

Everything that was lost in the garden will ultimately be restored when Jesus comes as Victorious King. There will be a perfect earth, perfect fellowship with God, and perfect relationships with others. Those who have chosen to live *in Jesus* will live forever as God intended. In His eternal kingdom there will be no more sin and no more death. Since we will be clothed in His perfect righteousness, there will be no more shame.

We, as brothers and sisters in Christ, will be joined with all the saints throughout the ages to live forever with Jesus in harmony and peace. We can be sure that this perfection will endure always because Satan, our Enemy — the tempter, deceiver, liar, and accuser — will be destroyed.

Jesus Christ, our *Sovereign King, Wisdom, Judge, Savior, Teacher,* and *Victorious King* is coming to reign supreme forever! What a promise! What a victory! What a King!

> And I saw heaven opened, and behold, a white horse, and He who sat on it is called Faithful and True, and in righteousness He judges and wages war. . . . He is clothed with a robe dipped in blood, and His name is called The Word of God. And the armies which are in heaven, clothed in fine linen, white and clean, were following Him on white horses. From His mouth comes a sharp sword, so that with it He may strike down the nations, and He will rule them with a rod of iron; and He treads the wine press of the fierce wrath of God, the Almighty. And on His robe and on His thigh He has a name written, "KING OF KINGS, AND LORD OF LORDS." (Revelation 19:11,13-16)

▶ The book of New Testament Prophecy shows Jesus as our **Victorious King**!

New Testament prophecy
Review/Discussion questions

(You may also use the Love & War Questions from your daily homework for discussion or review.)

1. What have you learned about God's glorious plan for the future?

2. What did you learn about God's books, or records, and His judgments?

3. What is the most important thing you have learned about Jesus?

4. What are you doing to prepare for Christ's return?

5. How has your life been changed through this study?

The end . . . but it is really just the beginning!

about the author

ELEANOR LEWIS is one of the four teachers of *The Amazing Collection: The Bible, Book by Book*, a DVD series produced by Big Dream Ministries that teaches the Bible in a sequential manner. She is also president of Insights and Beginnings, the producers of a DVD series that teaches how our temperament affects our everyday lives. Eleanor serves on the board of Big Dream Ministries and lives with her husband in Roswell, Georgia. She is the mother of a son and the grandmother of two boys.

about the teachers

PAT HARLEY has a master's degree in education from Western Michigan University and has taken courses from Dallas Theological Seminary. Pat was a cofounder of The Women's Fellowship and served as women's ministry director at Fellowship Bible Church in Roswell, Georgia. She is founder and president of Big Dream Ministries, Inc., producer of *The Amazing Collection: The Bible, Book by Book; The Amazing Adventure for children*; and *Invincible Love, Invisible War.*

DR. CRAWFORD LORITZ holds a bachelor of science degree from Philadelphia Biblical University, a doctor of divinity from Biola University, and a doctor of sacred theology from Philadelphia Biblical University. He has authored seven books and is presently senior pastor of Fellowship Bible Church in Roswell, Georgia. He is a visiting professor at Trinity Evangelical Divinity School. Crawford is the host of "Living a Legacy," a daily radio program, and has spoken for sports teams (at three Super Bowls), Promise Keepers, and senior military officers at the Pentagon.

ELEANOR LEWIS attended Pennsylvania State University and has an associate degree in business from Robert Morris University, but she has benefited most from her years as a student of God's Word! In addition to *Invincible Love, Invisible War*, she has written *How to Accept Yourself, Understand Others, and Like Them Anyway! A Study of the Personality Types*. Eleanor is also an inspirational speaker for conferences and retreats across America and internationally.

JOHN TURNER'S educational background includes studies at Pepperdine University, Pacific Christian College, and Bear Valley Bible Institute. He has studied theology, psychology, and philosophy, earning a ThM with an emphasis in New Testament Studies. He is currently pastor of Shannon Oaks Church in Sulphur Springs, Texas. John has coauthored three books with Dr. Ken Boa including a devotional titled *The 52 Greatest Stories of the Bible.*

LINDA SWEENEY attended Mississippi State University. She has taught in her church and community for many years and was a much-loved Bible Study Fellowship International teaching leader for eight years. Linda not only taught hundreds of women weekly but also invested herself in the lives of others by training a large number of BSFI leaders. She has taught women's retreats and conferences in the U.S. and Asia.

TOM JONES has a BBA degree from Hardin-Simmons University, Abilene, Texas, and a master of arts in religious education from Southwestern Baptist Theological Seminary, Ft. Worth, Texas. He presently serves as minister of education at Roswell Street Baptist Church in Marietta, Georgia. Tom has served churches in Texas and Georgia for more than thirty years and has led numerous education and equipping conferences.

ABOUT BIG DREAM MINISTRIES

Big Dream Ministries exists to help people understand the Bible as God's complete and amazing story of redemption through Jesus Christ and equip them to apply Biblical truths to their lives. We do this by offering studies that drive people to the Scriptures for answers and providing tools to reinforce the learning. Our vision is for people to be AMAZED by God's Word: to learn it, live it, and have it for life.

Our Collection of Bible Studies:

The Amazing Collection, The Bible, Book by Book
- Composed of 11 separate studies each teaching a section of the Bible. Together, *The Amazing Collection* covers every book of the Bible.
- Also available in Spanish (La Coleccion Maravillosa: La Biblia, Libro por Libro)

The Amazing Adventure
- An early childhood (3 – 7 years) curriculum with lessons, activities, and music to teach every book of the Bible

Be Amazing
- Based on Titus 2:3-5, this study teaches young women about godly character, healthy relationships, and managing a home.
- Also available in Portuguese (Seja Surpreendente: Estudo a luz da Biblia para a mulher surpreendente de hoje)

Invincible Love, Invisible War
- An excellent study for those who want to be prepared for spiritual battles by being armed with God's Word

The Amazing Temperaments
- This 6-week study biblically explores the strengths and weaknesses of each personality type to reach a full understanding and appreciation of yourself and others.

The Amazing Life of Jesus Christ, Part One and Part Two
- A chronological study of the Gospels that teaches about Christ's life in a deeper, more intentional way.

www.BigDreamMinistries.org

Made in United States
Orlando, FL
09 September 2023

36849317R10098